ESCAPE FROM ARNHEM

A Canadian Among the Lost Paratroops

Leo Heaps

SAPERE
BOOKS

ESCAPE FROM ARNHEM

Published by Sapere Books.

24 Trafalgar Road, Ilkley, LS29 8HH

United Kingdom

saperebooks.com

ISBN: 978-0-85495-097-3.

To
MY FATHER

TABLE OF CONTENTS

A NOTE ON ARNHEM   9
ESCAPE FROM ARNHEM   11
I   40
II   107
III: BELSEN   150
A NOTE TO THE READER 157

A NOTE ON ARNHEM

EIGHT THOUSAND MEN landed in the airborne army at Arnhem. Fifteen hundred recrossed the river on that fateful night of the evacuation. The total survivors finally amounted to two thousand. The true story of Arnhem is still being made. It is a tale told by one Dutchman to another, by one Dutch father to a Dutch son. It will be told by Dutchmen on winter evenings when the logs are burning on the hearth and Holland is at peace again.

Arnhem is the story of a people; one might say it is a saga of the Dutch nation. In those brief nine days everything in those four and a half years of Dutch struggle against an oppressing foe was brought to a climax. The history of the First Airborne Division will be written by able historians. It is the tale of a division reduced at times to a mere handful, struggling against German divisions; fighting tanks with machine-guns and hand grenades; of men attacking when they were considered beaten, counter-attacking until there was no one left to counter-attack; regiments wiped out and destroyed overnight; of a few men who held out on a bridge for a few days which seemed like an interminable hell. It is a tale told in deeds, not words. It is something intangible.

The great story, like most great stories, is the inconspicuous one. It is of the rising of the Dutch in Oosterbeek and Arnhem, of their eventual mutilation and death. Because for the Dutchman there is no such thing as being a prisoner. There is only freedom or death. The choice is plain. The Dutchman made up his mind. He fought until the end.

The Dutch Underground represents an army without uniform. They have few arms, few explosives. You might sometime ask a man from Arnhem what he thinks about the Dutch north of the Rhine. He will tell you. To him they are the finest people in the world.

ESCAPE FROM ARNHEM

IT ALL HAPPENED because I found Army life so difficult to adopt, and also because the Army found me at times to be somewhat of a problem child. I hoped that the answer to all my problems would be found in battle.

Here is how it began.

One day while lounging on my bed in a barrack room of our camp near Aldershot, Nova Scotia, my friend Gordon Roy looked down at me indifferently and said, "Do you know that the Canadians are loaning officers to the British Army? If you are accepted, you go within a month to England. It is the quickest way a fellow like you can get into action. Why don't you give it a go? All you have to do is to hand your name in to the Adjutant."

This sounded like the opportunity I had been waiting for, so that afternoon I handed my name in to the Adjutant and hoped that I would be accepted. Two weeks passed by and then one day while I was reading on the same bed, I was notified to quickly gather together my kit, as I was to move next morning to the depot where Canadian officers were to undergo special training before being loaned to the Imperial Army.

Our training centre was located in Sussex, New Brunswick. Here we underwent a special conversion course, to adjust ourselves as quickly as possible to British methods of Infantry warfare. And those in our group who had not been physically active during the past year were required to get into better physical trim. For one month we overcame obstacle courses, forded rivers and waded knee-deep in mire; and in turn I was overcome by a sprained ankle, a bad case of athlete's foot, and "pink eye". Time here was passing rapidly and the day was drawing near for our departure. And I was still confined to the hospital suffering from a myriad minor ailments.

The day before we were to leave camp for our embarkation port I was released from the hospital and was told that I would be leaving the next morning with the troop draft for England.

Our commanding officer, Brigadier Gregg, was the example that most officers at Sussex set before them. He had been awarded in the last war the Victoria Cross, Distinguished Service Order and the Military Cross. He was a man who was as humble as he was gallant and it was a fine experience to serve under him.

The night before we left he spoke to us of our responsibilities and obligations as junior officers, and there was a great understanding about the way he explained to us the business of war and its misfortunes. When he was through we packed our remaining items and went to bed, ready to leave early next morning for the docks of Halifax.

In two days we reached Halifax and boarded our ship. The voyage to me was a boring interval which I hoped would soon bring me closer and closer to the adventures of the battlefield. We were all very impatient and the ocean could not be crossed too soon to satisfy us.

Finally one afternoon after we passed around the top of Northern Ireland, through a murky fog we sighted land, and sailed down the west coast of Scotland, to emerge in the sunlight of Liverpool harbour later that same evening.

All day we waited restlessly aboard the ship. In the evening we disembarked into buses that were waiting for the Canadian officers on loan to the British. By bus we were taken to the station, where we immediately boarded a train for London.

Early next morning a horde of sleepy-eyed, wild, young Canadian officers went to the outside of Marylebone Station. They rubbed their eyes and gazed for the first time upon the immeasurable vastness of London.

Across from our railway station was the hotel where we were to stay until we left for our British regiments the following morning. London seemed gay, yet subdued. Scarred, yet the people miraculously thankful. So this was London. Most of us just walked and stared, like children being taken through the zoo.

It was with reluctance that we left the pubs, the cabbies, and our first taste of English courtesy. We had spoken that morning to women on the street with that gay abandon that novelty gives to you. We had walked for miles. We had bought sausage rolls and enjoyed them. We knew that in spite of our brief visit we could never forget London.

Then that afternoon we returned to the hotel and assembled in the large drawing-room to be instructed by an officer from the British War Office on our future moves.

I remember the officer who spoke to us. He was a rather pompous old British colonel with a bald crown which shone like polished ivory.

"My boys," he said, "evidently there is a fear among some of you about not arriving in time to see action. The reason for this loan of Canadian Army officers to the British Army is that our army is short of officers. D-Day is not far off. Some of you will be getting into regiments which may assault the beaches. Others will be getting into regiments whose task it will be to follow up those of you who will make the assault. But I can promise you all one thing, that you will all be in the hunt." That afternoon we were all assigned Divisions to report to the next day.

This was May 26, 1944.

Next morning our little group boarded the train and headed for our destination, somewhere in the south. All of us had been given the choice of joining the regiments we desired most to get into. Now we were actually on our way to fighting units, to work with men who had been trained to the highest combatant pitch and to see men who were experienced and wise in the ways of battle.

All through the morning our train pierced soft, wooded lands, and skirted the hills which lay as yielding as mounds of butter in the sun. The train flew on past a little hamlet, shining brightly in the morning, and then began to slow down, until it finally stopped at a tiny station tucked away in the southern county of Sussex. The land was beautiful to see this morning.

Here trucks and men to unload our baggage were waiting. We jumped on the trucks and in a minute were on our way on the next stage of our journey.

We arrived about noon at the headquarters of a British formation in the field. A real banquet had been prepared. We lunched in the best of comfort. The forty of us were told that we had the option of going to any battalion in the Division, providing too many of us did not favour any particular one. That afternoon the commander would address us, and formally welcome us to his division.

The morning passed very quickly in documentation. In the afternoon we were taken in trucks to the General's headquarters. We waited about on the lawn for him to appear. The general came out and received the salute from the group of Canadian subalterns who flocked about him.

He was an Englishman, bred in the musty tradition of Sandhurst. He carried a riding-crop in his left hand with which he nervously and occasionally whacked the right leg of his breeches. He had on an almost luminous pair of riding-boots, with two shining chopped spurs. His moustache was neither too long nor too short, and was meticulously groomed and waxed to perfection. His features were middle-aged, his dress was flawless. Behind him squatted a growling English bulldog.

"My Canadian officers," he began, "I always call the Canadian officers serving with me, 'my' Canadians. I am proud that you are to be in my division. Our role in this invasion, which is not very far off, is to break through the initial beach-head formed by the assault troops. We will break out of the beach-head, pass the assault troops by, and drive on to Berlin."

This seemed like quite a big job.

He really said much more, which I don't remember, but I was already growing impatient and was eager to move again. We were all very impatient and eager to set off on our next step, which would take us finally to our fighting battalions.

After the general was through, he wished us good luck, and we were left waiting for the trucks that were to transport us. There were three officers besides myself who were to go to a battalion called the Dorsets.

As we sat the in rear of the truck and watched the orchards and woodlands of Sussex slide past, I was filled with a breathless and unforgettable excitement. A sense told me for one brief moment of the thrilling times ahead, of the uncertainty of the future, and of a great adventure which was ours for the taking.

The Dorset Regiment is one of the oldest county regiments in England, and it is steeped in a tradition and history which are only matched by the ancient honours it has won from wars dating back almost to Cromwell's time. As yet we were ignorant of all these things, and we only knew that this Dorset battalion was our last stepping stone to the invasion coast of France.

When the truck stopped we found ourselves at a great rambling old house which was used as the officers' mess. This was to be my home for the next two weeks. The Colonel met us at the door and chatted amiably but briefly with us, and said he was glad that four Canadian officers were joining his regiment and hoped we would enjoy ourselves.

He was a young, regular soldier, and he breathed discipline.

The next morning the four of us visited the Colonel again, and he despatched each of us to a different part of the battalion to become acquainted with the methods used in training and their role as a unit in battle.

I was sent to the Bren-gun carriers, but the men here were much too busy to notice me. Everything was in a feverish state of preparation. New sides for waterproofing were being added to the carriers, so that when they drove off the assault barges water would not overflow the sides. Men were overhauling the motors, and each carrier held its battle complement of ammunition and explosives. Everybody and everything was almost ready for action.

As I was a surplus officer, I enjoyed the freedom of the battalion and often walked around the quaint little town of Bexhill where we were billeted, examining the barbed wire entanglements on the beaches and marvelling at the little lanes and drives overhung with thick elms which gave to this country so much of its charm. I used to stroll down to the sea where I could gaze on clear days across the Channel at the long, dark coast of France and say, to myself ... *how long now?*

Many of the men in the platoon I was attached to had been at Dunkirk, some had fought at El Alamein, and many were veterans of various other battles. I was totally inexperienced.

I used to listen to them talk, and all were generous and helpful. They complained about the uncertainty of their present status in the Army and told me how they wished a greater friendliness and understanding could be bred between officer and man. They were callous, but beneath their callousness there was a hidden warmth and a secret loneliness. Above all, they wanted friendliness and a little recognition, which most of them never seemed to receive.

One of the sergeants once said to me that the number of times you were in battle didn't necessarily contribute to your success as a leader in the field. If any officer in battle who met a crisis became master of the situation, his action would be almost automatic. There would be many who would not come up to the test of battle.

I listened and wondered. And I tucked these words away in the retainer of my brain.

That was June 1, 1944.

At the end of my short attachment to the Dorsets, Hal Foster, another Canadian and myself were called into the Colonel's office. The Colonel told us that, since there was no vacancy here for the two of us, we were to return to a British reinforcement unit, where we were to await further orders. For a moment all our hopes seemed shattered, all our dreams for D-Day gone. We were desolate as we left. Next day we boarded a train going north to London.

When we arrived at the reinforcement unit, which was located in some forgotten hamlet, we were told that we must move on again to another battalion of the Dorsets on the Thames Estuary near Gravesend, where we were to fill vacancies.

When we arrived at our new home we found it tense with expectancy. Preparations for invasion were visible here also.

Perhaps we would not be disappointed. We were no longer quite so downcast at the thought of not seeing action. We began to brighten up. It looked like we were in a fine unit.

As usual when we arrived at a new British unit we were treated with a detached indifference. There was always considerable difficulty in finding out just how we were to be disposed of.

Wherever Hal and I went, we were looked upon as two lost Canadian officers. Always we had to go through the long procedure of identification, and explanation as to what we were doing in the British Army. As a result, most of our time with the British Army was spent on leave in London avoiding these questions. Occasionally we would spend a day at camp, only to find that it would be unnecessary.

I met a great many very pleasant English officers, and made the observation that really our ways of living were not so very different. And that beneath all the little mannerisms of some, and the excessive politeness of others, we had really much in common.

One evening Hal and I were stopped while walking in the village by one of the English officers from our camp, and he asked if we would drop in a little pub for a glass of beer. We accepted. He was a tall thin Oxford graduate who seemed to have a permanent fixture in one eye to receive a monocle.

"You know," the Englishman said, "it is a fine idea that Canadians should volunteer to serve with our regiments. A fine idea."

"We are glad to do it," we replied. "Besides, it provides us with a chance to do something worthwhile."

"Obviously you have never been to battle before. It is not quite as exciting as you think," the Englishman smiled.

We looked at the campaign ribbons on his chest.

"You needn't worry about missing out," he continued. "The division you are in now," and he leaned over closer to us, "happens to be the assault division." Then he whispered, "The brigade you are in happens to be at the spearhead of the division, and your battalion is the spearhead of the brigade. So you really shouldn't worry, should you?"

"Oh!" we said.

We all got up and went out to the already darkening evening. The next morning we went on leave to London again.

If I seem to talk a great deal about getting into action, it is not because we were great adventurers who would like to continually hazard the unknown. It is only because normally in the Army you are confronted with a terrible boredom — a great desire to give expression to all those things which live inside you. You have a yearning to break away from routine and regulations. We all dreamed that battle would be our salvation. And in some mysterious way we hoped that we would all have a great adventure. (Most of us did.) This was our dream.

While Hal and I were on leave in London we received one morning a telegram instructing us to report back to camp immediately.

When we arrived in camp the air bristled with electricity. Almost as soon as we entered the camp gates an orderly rushed up to us and said we were to report to the orderly-room immediately. In the orderly-room the Adjutant said that they had been looking for the two of us for three days, and that we were now confined to camp. We must be ready to leave the camp at 0400 hours two days hence.

"Where are we going?" we asked.

"You are going to war."

This was June 3, 1944.

The next day passed by without us being aware of very much except packing the essentials and discarding the rest of our belongings. Then in the next cold, brittle dawn we boarded a train. Each man was laden with his battle order. We were told that we were headed for a port in south-east England. A mile or two from the port of embarkation we assembled at a camp which was specially prepared for the assault troops. No one was allowed to leave or re-enter the camp. Here we underwent our final rehearsal for the great day which was so very near. We were issued with special additional equipment. And I went to have my athlete's foot treated. It bothered me.

That night in a dimly lit tent we underwent our final briefing. We were told by Intelligence officers the latest information concerning the strength of the German units we were most likely to meet. Our objectives were memorized from aerial photographs and our roles committed to our memories.

The Engineers were to land in our sector of the beach just before we were to go ashore, and lay two white tapes which would indicate a cleared lane through the minefields. All the time there would be continuous air support. To the left of us would be the Canadian division, to the right another British division. The details were finally ironed out, and minor difficulties overcome. Then I was told the serial number of the ship that was to take us into striking distance of the shore, and the number of the assault craft with which we were to storm the beach. It was now eleven o'clock at night, and reveille was at 0400 hours the following morning. I went to bed.

Next morning we marched the mile to the docks, and passed on the way silent columns of our troops who were manning the lines of supply. The area was forbidden to civilians. When we arrived at the dock we lay on the cold cement floor, waiting. Presently through the blurred morning air we could see a ship coming in to dock. Hanging from the sides were the assault craft with which we would storm the beaches.

We talked of everything. Of home, of tomorrow, yesterday, and what the battle was to be like for the first time. We talked furiously. Some of the men slept, others feigned sleep. A nervous glint shone from the eyes of some. Others had a visible tremor. Some were as cool and collected as others were fearfully expectant of the battle.

The big ship had docked now. The little assault craft hanging from its sides were trim and freshly painted in blue camouflage. The crew, leaning over the ship's side, were tired and grimy. They grinned at us and shouted how they would put the first wave ashore on the beaches as if it was a Sunday excursion to Calais.

Then we went up the gangplank aboard the ship. There was a little singing but not very much.

The ship was delightful. We had cabins with hot and cold running water, and superb meals. It all seemed so incongruous, so unreal. Here we were on our way across the Channel to be launched in assault boats in a few hours against the enemy, and now we were living in unbelievable comfort aboard a Liberty Ship.

I went to supper that night with Hal and surprised myself by having a big appetite. We were all hungry, and we ate in a meditative silence. But I do not think that our hunger was for food. We ate because a strange tension rested upon us, and a terrible loneliness was gnawing at our hearts. Our hunger for the fight was changing now that we were very near to it. It was changing into I know not what. It was almost a detached religious calm. Since we did not know exactly what it was that bothered us, we ate with fury.

That night after I turned out the cabin light and went to bed, I looked out of the opened porthole across the star-lit waters, and saw a great convoy of ships at my side. I was no longer lonely, and I went to sleep.

We were awakened early, very early. The loudspeaker was bawling 314K … 314K. That was our serial number. We jumped into our clothes, strapped on our battle-gear, and checked our weapons. When we reached the deck, the crews were already in the assault craft. Some of the motors were being rehearsed. Other assault craft were in the water. Somebody was shouting that once you were on the beach you must be sure to follow the white tape through the minefield.

A naval officer tapped me gently on the shoulder and said, "Your men are already in the craft; you shove off first. Good luck, old man."

I was now fairly calm, except for that little knot of suppressed excitement which hung just above the belly. I stepped into the assault craft. All the other men were already in it. We were lowered into the water. The boat lines were disengaged. The motors roared and we were away. For the first time the German shore battery shelled us. I looked behind me, and I saw Hal in his craft. We were still together.

It was light now and the beach was half a mile or less away. With my binoculars I could make out a ripped landing craft lying turned over on the sand, a burned-out Churchill tank which had been struck by an anti-tank shell, and saw the bursts from a German shore-battery landing close to the larger ships of our convoy. I could see, too, a few bodies lying on the sands, and the living working among them. I put down my binoculars and waited.

There were plenty of our aircraft overhead diving and picking off, like huge falcons, enemy strongpoints. It seemed as if the Germans had moved well back from the yellow sands to the green country beyond. It could have been a beautiful morning.

The assault craft jarred to a stop on the sand. The front came down. We plunged down the gangplank into three feet of water, and followed the white tape up the beach to the little road which would take us to Audrieu. Everywhere there seemed to be chaos. Somebody sprayed us with a burst of machine-gun fire. We quickly flattened ourselves on the ground and waited. Presently the machine-gun stopped. We got up and moved on again. There were no casualties, and everybody was very alert.

On the little road which passed by Audrieu we stopped at a French café. Someone inside insisted that we drink to "France Libre". We did. The people were sitting around little wooden tables like their ancestors had been doing for hundreds of years. You saw no particular display of emotion. All of it burned from the inside. Everything about them seemed to tell of some sort of quiet suffering. Some, I think, feared the hand of the Allies. None knew what their future would be. Their homes were in ruins and afire in their native land. Their farms had been pillaged and their stores of food ravaged by the Germans. Yet in some of their eyes one might, if one looked closely, see a happy little glow.

A mile behind me on the beaches, huge supplies of all kinds were being brought in. All over the sands food, machines, and ammunition was piling up.

I moved on down the road heading south, searching for someone who could tell me where the main body of my regiment was. I met a strolling colonel who instructed me to find a place to sleep that night with my men along the side of the road. Early next morning, he told me, I was to be picked up and would join my battalion who were now riding on the tanks, and were too far away for me to reach that night.

That afternoon we took up a position around a big French farm and tried to engage the escaped Russian prisoners in conversation. We collected eggs in exchange for chocolate, and spoke our very best French to the locals. When evening drew in about us we returned to our farm where we had dug our slit-trenches, and I ordered a "stand to", which meant nobody slept that night more than an hour or two. The only German opposition was two lonely snipers who fired occasionally in our direction before, I imagine, they went to bed for the night.

Early next morning I discovered, parked on the road which ran by the farmhouse, a lost truck containing two Canadians from the Third Division. The driver of the vehicle did not know where he was or where he had come from. He had driven up from the south yesterday and was quite unaware that for a day he had been circulating in German territory. He was quite happy, however, to see us. We borrowed his truck, piled in the back, and headed due south along a little side road. I noticed many dead bodies about. The smell of rotting human flesh mingled strangely with the sweet perfume of the lilacs. Many of our paratroopers lay where they had come down, and beside some of them there were little dried pools of blood.

At last we came to a house which was occupied by some of our own troops. A lieutenant in charge told me I was insane to have come down the road we were on, as all that morning there had been heavy fighting on either side. Since we were ignorant of this fact, fate seemed to have treated us kindly. The Lieutenant gave me some more directions. Then we sped on down the road amidst an ever-increasing crunch of mortars and whirr of machine-gun bullets, until we gained the centre of a little wooden perimeter. Here, amidst the trees, were the tanks and men of my regiment. All of us were very glad to see them.

I went to the Colonel. He told me what had happened since the landing. They had been ordered to join the tanks as a protective element to help eliminate small pockets which contained German eighty-eight millimetre guns. Casualties had been heavy, as they had been exposed most of the day yesterday to German crossfire.

The Colonel was clean-shaven and fresh, but when you took a second glance his bloodshot eyes gave him away. Lt.-Col. Norey was a fine man. Everybody, who had ever worked with him, respected him. He had been on Montgomery's staff in Africa and had asked for a field appointment. Now he asked me to see the Adjutant.

The Adjutant was a young Englishman, suave, uncertain; he had obviously been more than a little shaken since the initial landing. He was very tired. In fact, no one in the battalion had rested in forty-eight hours. The Adjutant informed me that yesterday morning the Intelligence officer had been killed, and I was to take his place. The Adjutant instructed me where to bed down and where I could find Lt.-Col. Norey. Then he left me alone in the shellfire.

An Intelligence officer in an infantry battalion does not have a pleasant job to perform. In fact, it is a very busy occupation. Often he must lead the attack when there is any doubt about the direction of the enemy. He must correlate the enemy position with our own, and he must have all the latest data and all recent changes in the advance ready to give to the officers and N.C.O.s at any time during the day or night. Much worse than this, however, was the fact that Intelligence officers of Infantry battalions are very expendable.

My qualifications for this job were non-existent. Except once I was almost accepted for an Intelligence course, but was returned without a second consideration to normal soldiering. There was a lull now in the battle, and night was settling upon the treetops and upon the ground.

"What do you want me to do, sir?"

I looked down and realized I was not alone. Standing beside me was a tiny Cockney. He could not have been more than five foot one inch in height.

"Who are you?" I asked.

"I'm Martin, your batman. Your bed is down there in the ditch." With this he pointed an invisible hand in the night. Then added, "If you want me, I'll be sleeping."

With this short statement he left me and I began to wander around our position in the dark. The half-moon glowed weakly through a cloud. I could hear the sharp, ear-splitting crack of the self-propelled guns behind me shelling their night target. The guns moved closer in my direction. Presently the Adjutant bumped into me. He was excited.

"The Boche are forming up for an attack on Dog Company. We're trying to break it up with the artillery."

"Where is Dog Company?" I asked.

"About twenty yards on your right." He threw a hand out into the night in the general direction of the right, and was gone.

I could hear him bellowing out orders in the dark, and saw shapes rustling by the bushes going vaguely in the direction of Dog Company. All that night there was a stand to. The Germans were drawing very close to us. No one dared sleep.

Toward dawn the fervour of the battle increased. The air was laced with the quick, sudden fire of Spandaus. Then our own Bren guns would beat out a slow, but steady reply. Next our

Vickers machine-guns would join in, with a steady stream of machine-gun bullets whistling through the branches overhead. In a moment our self-propelled guns began a rapid fire, which was interspersed with the far-distant cracking of the big-calibre naval guns firing from the ships lying off shore. It was a symphony of war. The Germans began to shell us in return. A German eighty-eight shell landed just behind me. There were casualties. You could hear the wounded groan and see them twitch. Beside the wounded some dead lay still.

The Colonel came up to me and told me to follow him. Together we went out to the forward companies' slit-trenches. I was to inspect the positions and collect intelligence. As we approached one of the slit-trenches a lieutenant wearily crawled out of it and came toward us. It was Hal Foster. I was very glad to see him. Evidently he had arrived before me and had been with the regiment from the very beginning. Hal's normally jovial face was grimmer than I had ever seen it. When he made his usual funny remarks he didn't smile like he used to. His stocky body didn't look comfortable in these foreign surroundings and he appeared ill at ease with the Colonel. Hal looked a bit ashen around the jaw. And his movements were slow because his limbs were heavy with fatigue. We wished each other good luck, and then I moved on with the Colonel.

"You know," the Colonel said, "that other Canadian," and he pointed back to Hal, "is the most forward officer in the British Army today."

The Colonel confided in me that our position was extremely hazardous. The battalion, he said, had moved too rapidly, and left no lines of supply behind. Evidently the regiment of tanks was operating with our battalion under Lt.-Col. Norey's command, and he had orders to hold the high ground until tomorrow morning.

When we had finished our rounds, the Colonel introduced me to the Brigadier who had attached his Brigade Headquarters to our regimental headquarters. Then I was left alone to observe what I could.

Everybody I noticed was on thin edge, and could not sleep for more than a few minutes at a time. I decided to walk around with the Intelligence sergeant. We ended up near a little clump of bushes on a high piece of ground near the place I had inspected this morning. Here we took up a good position for observation. About two hundred yards ahead a cloud of dust spiralled up into the sky. Then other clouds joined the first. These were enemy tanks.

Nearby the motors of our tanks began to roar as they moved out of the trees and across the open ground to engage the enemy. The outline of our Sherman tanks was broken by camouflaging of pine-trunks and tank-treads, which were secured to the side and front of each tank. The Shermans gathered speed as they lumbered down the gentle slope to meet the enemy.

In the distance two tanks had already been hit, and oily flames spurted from the turrets. From each of the hit tanks grimy-faced tank-men scrambled out and ran for their lives into the bushes nearby.

About two hundred yards ahead of me I studied with my binoculars the tanks moving in and out of the narrow streets of the village of Villers Bocage. German and English tanks were fighting it out among the ruined houses of this tiny hamlet. One tank was indistinguishable from the other in the mêlée of the battle. Our artillery was firing smoke ahead of our tanks so that they might be obscured from the enemy. Around me the German shells were bursting with increased fury. Machine-gun slugs were splattering and flattening out the little risings on the level ground. You could see the little metal bullets glisten in the sun. The battle in the village ahead was hidden by clouds of smoke and columns of dust which settled gently over everything.

I wrote a few observations and handed the paper to the Sergeant, who left me to take the report back to the Colonel. As I lay in my little clump of bushes I tried hard to make sense out of what I saw. The harder I tried, the more entangled I became. I decided then that the only way to treat the fighting of war was as a costly and extravagant game. It certainly was the most exciting game I had ever known.

Later on I returned to our battalion headquarters to find out how the battle was going on the other battalion fronts. Everything seemed to be going satisfactorily. About four o'clock that afternoon some of the tanks had returned from the village. Out of the thirty-five tanks which went out, fifteen survived to return. There were many wounded to look after, but there was hardly time.

The air was filled with the bursts of many machine-guns as if the German Army in this area had unleashed upon us all its fury. It was a steady blur of noise. Men began dropping silently and quickly. I dove into a slit-trench. Inside I discovered a captain who had been directing the naval guns, firing from off shore, until now. He was compressed against the bottom of the slit-trench like a pad. He cushioned my dive.

Presently I crawled out of the slit-trench and went to look for the Colonel. Somebody was shouting for me. It was the Adjutant. Evidently the Colonel had been looking for me, but I could not find him. People were shouting that eight German tanks were approaching our perimeter from all sides, and the tanks were accompanied by German Infantry. I had to take charge, it seemed, of the side of the perimeter that I was on; I began to organize it for defence. I met a calm sergeant and put him in charge while I went to look for the Colonel.

When I returned to the position that I had been observing from this afternoon there were many bodies lying about. One hundred yards away from here I could see kicked-up dust following in the wake of German tanks. Near me were Infantry men manning the slit-trenches with their bazookas and machine-guns, waiting for the German tanks and Infantry to come into sight. There was nobody I wanted around here, so I returned to the headquarters to look for my Intelligence sergeant.

At the headquarters I found Martin, my batman. I had not seen him since the evening he had joined me.

"I've been here waiting for you," he said. He pointed to a slit-trench almost completely hidden by a clump of bushes.

"Wait in the same place for me," I said. When I later had time to return Martin had vanished and I never saw him again.

After a little searching I found the Intelligence sergeant. He was lying with his notebook in one hand and a pencil in the other. He had been trying to write the Intelligence summary for the day, but he would never complete it. He had been struck down by shrapnel from an air-bursting shell, and the side of his head had been half torn away.

For a moment I was very frightened. But then fear passed off as quickly as it had come. In its place was left a peculiar emptiness. At such a time the most hideous things seem to assume the qualities of everyday occurrences.

In front of me, on the border of a little ridge of trees, the Major, who was the second-in-command of our battalion, was walking nonchalantly up and down. Everyone else was scraping the bottom of their slit-trench. The Major twirled his long waxed moustache and blinked his baby blue eyes. Machine-gun bullets whizzed around him. Every now and then he would thump his cane impatiently on the ground in an effort to exhort the men. I thought that he was very daring, until I learned that he was suffering from what is known as being "bomb-happy", which is the same thing as being "punch-drunk". How he was not killed that day I will never know. This man lived not only to do this in future battles, but also lived to command the battalion. He was a courageous person.

A few minutes later I met the Adjutant again, and he pointed a few yards away to the Intelligence sergeant, and said that I must take from him the Intelligence map. The Sergeant looked ghastly. I felt my stomach sinking again, and tried to slip back inconspicuously out of the way of the air-bursting shells and machine-gun fire. However, I forced myself to crawl over and remove the map from out of his blood-soaked tunic. After I took out the map, I returned to take over from the Sergeant I had left in charge of my side of the perimeter. I met the naval Captain again and together we planned how we would hold this position when the German attack came that night.

I could see the stretcher-bearers taking the wounded and putting them on ambulances. The ambulances were leaving the perimeter and heading north toward the beach-head. There were a great many more wounded than I thought. The summer night had already begun to descend.

All that night we waited for the German attack to come, but it never did. The only excitement was when a German tank indifferently lumbered through our headquarters. Somebody, mistaking it for one of our tanks, tried to slow it down. The tank stopped, shot up the Brigade Headquarters, and passed on through. Fortunately, no one was hurt.

The morning found me cold, covered with dirt, miserable. The other Captain was still asleep when I awoke and crossed the ditch to report to our battalion headquarters, from which, all night long, I had been separated by a ditch and a clump of trees. It seemed that runners had been looking for me during the night, but couldn't find me. Everybody was annoyed with me except the Colonel, who appeared almost pleased. This made me feel much better. We were to rest for the remainder of the morning and before noon were to move off to a new position from which we could begin the day's attack.

The stretcher-bearers brought in about two dozen stretchers and deposited them on the ground in even rows. Each body was carefully covered by a drab grey Army blanket. The Adjutant was removing the identification from around each man's neck. The doctor, visibly shaken from the previous night, was certifying the bodies dead. Someone else was removing weapons and items of equipment that might be useful to other people. The dead lay very quiet, and yet there seemed so much left for them to say. It was difficult to understand right away why this had happened. I was very uneasy, for no one ever gets used to their own dead. Inside me a pent-up feeling, half of fear, and half of uncertainty, prevented me from resting.

I knew that on one of those stretchers was a young English lieutenant whom I had spoken to yesterday. He had shown me a picture of his wife from Manchester, and his young child. Now I looked at his boots. That was all I could look at — a pair of mud-plastered boots lying at a very awkward angle on the stretcher. I got up and wandered back to where the Colonel was. I didn't want to think of what might have happened to Hal Foster.

In an hour we were to move off, and as Intelligence officer, I was to lead the battalion in a Bren-gun carrier to our next objective. The objective was just a point on the map to me, and my method of getting there would be the shortest distance between two points.

Finally, after a half an hour's search I discovered my carrier. Behind it twenty vehicles were lined up, and behind the vehicles were the remnants of the battalion. Even now the column seemed to stretch for miles, and it appeared that everybody was waiting for me. I was much too tired to care about how I was to arrive at our destination, or how long it would take me to get there.

That morning one of the most peculiar columns I had ever seen started off on a journey, the like of which I never want to see again. We started off across fields, went through woods, over hills. And no matter where I went, the rest of the column followed. I went through minefields, within whistling distance of German positions. We were shelled, mortared, and machine-gunned. The track came off my carrier, and the vehicles had flat tyres. We backed up and went forward again. But, miracle of miracles, we arrived four hours later at our destination.

My column swept by a burnt-out tank, still smouldering from the morning battle, and I was directed at this spot by a very meticulous Military Policeman, resplendent in his white belt and creased trousers, into a wooded enclosure. Beside a battered old house stood the Brigadier. He directed us into the rambling old manor, and we stood amazed. Before our eyes was a table set in the creamy whiteness of the finest French linen. The table held an abundance of food. Roast meats, fresh green garden vegetables, luscious red grapes fairly bursting in our sight, and decanters of wine. Behind the table stood our gracious French hosts. An old man and woman who beckoned us to eat. We needed no second invitation.

"We are very glad to see you," said the old Frenchman. His wife nodded and smiled. "We have not very much, but what we have, you are welcome to."

His home had been plundered by the Germans. His orchards were destroyed by the tanks, his fields of corn set afire by the flame-throwers, and the wheat had been trampled down to the earth by the marching feet of the Infantry men. But he had managed to hide some food and wine in the cellar. From this stock they fed us. We returned their kindness by giving them canned foods and chocolate. It was such a pity to see these fine people reduced to this state of poverty.

All the time the troops and the tanks and the supplies were streaming in, and seemed to make a desert out of a paradise. In later days I knew that these people came to understand why this was. They knew that once again France had become the inevitable battlefield. And they accepted everything in their understanding French way.

After lunch everyone had a short rest and my little section literally slept under the barrels of some field-guns which began firing. We were too tired to be bothered by them.

I watched the face of the Colonel as he slept. He was deep in sleep, yet his face was terribly awake. It had about it a twitch which contracted the portion from his left ear to his chin. And from between closed lips there came occasionally short and painful cries. The strain of battle could never leave his body. It would be with him for the rest of his days. His face was gaunt and intelligent in appearance, and in his waking hours it was calm and placid as a summer lake. Now the curtain on his face had been lifted and it was bare of all protection. On it were little squirming figures of pain and suffering. In the field he was always the model of bravery. (When he was killed later by a stray burst of machine-gun fire, each man in the battalion lost a little part of himself.) I could sleep no longer, so I rose and went down the road to look for Hal.

I found him resting in a little French farmhouse a few hundred yards from me. He was well, and his usual congenial self again. It was good to meet another Canadian like Hal. In the attack last night half of his platoon had been wiped out, and Hal had several very narrow escapes himself. He had adopted a very fatalistic outlook. I told him that we would move in one hour. He walked back down the road with me. It was a hot dusty day, and every step we took raised a little puff of dust as high as our knees. A despatch rider drove up to me and said that I was to report back to the Colonel immediately. The last words I heard Hal say as I left were, "If I get through this afternoon, I'll be bloody lucky."

Everybody was awake and ready for the move.

As we advanced down the road in column, we passed burnt-out hulls of tanks, dead Germans in the ditch and bloated and putrefying horses. We went through the narrow streets of a tiny village with gutted houses on either side. I could see no civilians about. They had wisely taken to the fields and the woods. There seemed to be no Germans here to oppose us. Soon we reached a crossroad and stopped by the side of the road to consult our maps. We turned left at the crossroads and reached our position for the night. It was an open field with a few trees scattered on it.

That night we were warned that a great bombing attack involving hundreds of aircraft was to take place a mile ahead of us, the purpose being to soften up enemy strongpoints which we were to advance on next day. This attack was to take place at ten o'clock the following morning.

Next morning at ten o'clock one lone Spitfire strafed an unknown enemy position ahead. We waited for an hour for the rest of the aircraft to appear, but none came. We knew now that we had had our air support. Then our attack started.

The three companies of our battalion moved in three columns into the attack. I moved with the centre column. Our artillery was falling short and many of our soldiers were struck down by our own shells. We saw only a few Germans in the woods, and, except for the odd sniper who fired occasionally at us, opposition was light. However, the companies on the flanks suffered many casualties from German mortar and machine-gun fire. All that afternoon we advanced slowly and carefully up the dust-choked road. When the sun began to set we stopped for the night, and I watched the wounded and the dead returning on the stretchers.

During the night we kept a strict vigilance because German tanks were patrolling the vicinity. The night was alive with tracers whizzing from the German positions across the sky, and the darkness was lit by the brilliance of flares both from ourselves and the enemy.

Next morning the battalion rested. I gathered around my little section and together we made the necessary reports which I had to hand in to Brigade Headquarters. On the road there were a great many dead Germans killed by our artillery fire. Some of the Germans clutched in their hands small vials of acid, which they had intended to throw through the slit-holes of our tanks. Others lay where they had fallen beside their guns. All the Germans seemed to be very well equipped.

I had been told by the Colonel of our battalion that he had seen about twenty Canadians who had been shot by the Germans after they had been taken prisoner. This had occurred on D-Day. The courtyard where those Canadians had been murdered was located in the little village of Audrieu, which was a very short distance from where I was now. I decided to go and verify this for myself.

When I arrived in Audrieu the bodies were still untouched. It was obvious they had been lined up against the wall and shot. The dead men lay like twisted ragdolls, and some of them had been shot many times. This was war in all its horror. I knew the flesh was beginning to rot because an awful stench rose from the bodies. None of our little party spoke as we left. We knew that the German SS were the people responsible for this atrocity.

During the next two days the battalion took up a defensive position on the side of a hill, which overlooked a great stretch of Normandy farmlands.

Everywhere the countryside was blooming, and the grasses were singing in the summer winds. Everyone slept long hours. The men were very tired. Reinforcements came up during the day, and the battalion was slowly coming up to strength.

You could see the Frenchmen returning home from their dug-outs in the fields now that the waves of battle had passed. They were going back to their smouldering houses.

Whenever we visited the people they offered us wine and talked about the four years of occupation they had undergone. These people seemed to accept things very philosophically, picked up their ploughs and harnessed what horses had not been killed by the artillery, and began once again to till the fields and cultivate the land for food. They had suffered more than man could know, and yet they returned to their homes and began to live again.

Two days later the Germans began to shell our positions. The Adjutant was hit and had to be evacuated. One whole section of machine-gunners were casualties. All during the day we were shelled periodically by heavy-calibre guns.

In order to walk from where I was bivouacked, to the battalion headquarters, it was necessary to cross an open space of ground about fifty yards across. I had crossed it several times during the day, and decided that I would visit the battalion headquarters once again. Halfway across the field I heard the whine of a big shell, and flung myself to the ground. The air was rent by a great explosion, and I seemed to be enveloped by a yellow flame. It was all very brief. The blast threw me about five feet in the air but when I landed I was only slightly dazed by the concussion, and perfectly all right otherwise. I arose and continued to walk to battalion headquarters.

Later on that day I decided I would visit a medical dressing station which was camped only one hundred yards away. The medical officer took one look at me and said that he would give me a sedative and I was to rest here for the night. I persisted in saying that I felt well, but agreed to stay that night. The sedative began to work and I fell quickly into a deep, untroubled sleep.

When I awoke next morning I realized that the machinery of evacuation had begun to work. It was like being on an assembly line. It seemed that during the night I had passed back from one medical station to another until now I was on my way by ambulance to the beach-head. From here I was to be removed back to England on a tank-landing craft.

I began to protest to the orderly and he returned with the medical officer. Both agreed that it was acute shock. The more I protested, the more critical the doctor seemed to think that my condition was, until finally he thought I was delirious. At last I submitted. It would not be of any use to say any more to the attendants. However, I was determined that I would return soon. But yet, in a way, I was glad to be going back to England.

Little did I know then that the experiences of these last twelve days were only a prelude to a much greater adventure, which I would embark upon in the near future.

I

IT WAS NO TROUBLE to get discharged from the hospital. I was much too healthy to take up the time of the nurses and the doctors. I caused a minor scandal one day by walking across the road to a Canadian quartermaster store where I was outfitted with a complete new uniform, which seemed to me to be a pleasant contrast to the drab blue hospital dress. Next day the Colonel of the hospital called me in. He told me the people were now casting aspersions as to the considerateness of the hospital staff. After that my fate was sealed. If one could possibly have got a dishonourable discharge from the hospital, I'm sure that I did.

Next day I left for an Infantry holding unit.

For a long period I was shuttled between one holding unit and another without being given any specific job. Life for me had now become one prolonged period of waiting. After several weeks of this I made application to join the British Paratroops. Then I underwent another period of waiting. Two weeks later, I was told to report to an officers' selection board which was designed for the sole purpose of recruiting paratroop officers. The period of selection was to be over two days during which all the selectees were to undergo various psychologically designed tests. These two days were among the oddest I had ever spent in any one place in my life.

Everywhere I went I was followed by a long-moustached instructor who peeked out from behind corners and trees, scribbling in a notebook my every move and gesture. I was confronted by such a baffling assortment of questions and proposals that I found difficulty in treating anything seriously. I found myself crawling through barrels, under tarpaulin, and answering a thousand different questions concerning every relevant and irrelevant phase of my life. As far as I could discover the primary object of this course was to impress the very dapper-looking Colonel who was in charge. I failed to impress him.

Two weeks later I learned from the holding unit I was with that I had failed to pass. I became very annoyed and indignant. As a result of all this I stamped my way to the War Office in Whitehall and knocked on the door of a General's secretary, and to my amazement was immediately granted an interview with the General in charge of Airborne training. The General was a very kind and considerate man, who listened to my story with a great deal of sympathy. Here, I thought, was someone who might be good enough to help me.

"My boy," the General began, "I jumped, myself, into France on D-Day and I am almost fifty years old. If I can do it, I know you can." Then he added, with a little twinkle in his eye, "What do you think of the paratroop selection board for officers?"

I told him that they didn't impress me very much. And that naturally they didn't have to.

"Well, boy, if I went there, I would probably fail myself," he confided in me. "Don't worry about it, I'll do my best to see that you are transferred directly to a paratroop battalion. Leave your particulars behind."

I left happy. Here was someone at last who would help me to do what I wanted to do most in the Army — join the paratroops.

This was the first of August.

One sultry day three weeks later, when time was hanging heavy on my hands, I was called into the orderly-room.

The Adjutant handed me a transportation warrant.

"Heaps, you are to report immediately to the First British Paratroop battalion at this address in Lincolnshire." He gave me the address on a slip of paper. Then he added, "It seems as if someone in the War Office has been pulling for you."

The next day I arrived at Bourne in the lovely county of Lincolnshire. I was met at the station and driven through a land brown with autumn to a castle where the battalion was billeted. Here I met Lt.-Colonel Dobie, D.S.O., who was the commanding officer. I met the other officers and men and was immediately affected by the great sense of camaraderie and keenness which was in the battalion. The officers were good, and the men were real fighting men who knew their job. I knew I would enjoy every minute here, even though I was the only Canadian officer in the battalion. The equipment I was issued with was the best, and there were special issues of weapons and wearing apparel which I had never seen before. There was an *esprit de corps* about, which infected the very marrow in your bones, and compelled you almost to be off for new adventure.

I learned that twelve separate airborne operations had already been proposed. Some of these were to have taken place in France and Belgium. But each operation was cancelled just before the proposed deadline. Now things were quiet and the men waited, and the people in the village of Bourne knew that the men were waiting. Everyone knew that sooner or later there would be an operation which would not be cancelled.

After only one week the seed of a new operation had begun to grow at Airborne Headquarters. Finally the completed Operational Order was handed down to us. This time we were to land on the east side of the Leopold Canal in Belgium, and would cut off the Germans fleeing to the east. That night the radio news informed us that our troops had already crossed the Leopold Canal in strength and were pushing still farther eastward. We knew that this operation would be cancelled, and that next day our Belgian francs would be handed back to the paymaster.

The next operation planned was to take place on the Dutch-Belgium frontier. For days we scrutinized aerial photographs, were briefed twice daily and studied on the sand-table the contours and topographical features of the ground we would drop on, and operate in. Everybody, in his mind's eye, knew his job. Everyone down to the last man repeated his task back to his officer. And each officer repeated in turn on the sand-table his job to the Colonel. The planes were assigned to each stick, and all knew the order of the flight. I was to jump in the first lift in one of the Headquarter Company planes. I was assigned to collect all transport I could find with the aid of a batman who would jump behind me. Two hours before we were to embus for the airport everything was cancelled. Our statachutes were turned in, and everybody went on two days' leave. (Statachutes are parachutes which open automatically and are used by all paratroops.)

When I returned from my leave the atmosphere had grown tense again. The air was humming with a suppressed excitement. The sand-table in the operations room was remoulded to represent new terrain. New aerial photographs were received, new maps of Holland were issued, and new Dutch money was given to us. We tried on different statachutes, chalked our names on them and piled them in our correct jumping-sticks.

On Friday night we were briefed. When the Intelligence officer read us the enemy strength, everybody laughed a little. Our strength was seven thousand men. To the west of the area we were to drop in the Germans had several tank divisions, to the east they had some Infantry divisions, and to the north they had a huge SS troop-training centre around Amsterdam. Two American airborne divisions would land to our south; one at Eindhoven, and the other at Nijmegen. Our job was to close the escape route north of the Rhine to the Germans, who would try to flee eastward from our ground troops.

The First British Airborne Division, of which my battalion was a part, was to drop north of a place on the lower Rhine known as Oosterbeek. We were then to march seven miles east to take a town called Arnhem. My battalion was to be the first to drop on Sunday, 17 September. The British Airborne Division would be separated by the Rhine from the Americans twenty-five miles to the south. It was a daring plan. But our Colonel told us to treat it like we had treated the others. It was another exercise which was sure to be cancelled as all the rest had been. Since the divisional staff were running out of code names for operations, this was known by no name, except Operation Arnhem.

Saturday came. I tried out my new tommy-gun, and then wrote a few farewell letters as I had done so many times before, but took the precaution of not mailing them. After each cancellation I would apologize to my friends when I saw them, and have to answer embarrassing questions about why I wrote such letters. This time, I decided, would be the last time I would undertake to write. From now on I would only write when the operation was completed.

One of my good friends in the battalion was Eric Davies, a lieutenant, who had given up the ballet to join the paratroops. He had won the Military Cross in Italy the year before, after he had escaped from the Germans. Now he took war calmly and was inclined to be a little sceptical, and together we planned our next leave in London after the cancellation came through.

Saturday midnight came and there was no cancellation. I checked my equipment very carefully and had a long talk with my batman about the job we were to do. Reveille was at five o'clock the next morning, and we were to leave for the airport at eight o'clock. I was tired, and went to bed and slept well. I dreamed about the elaborate preparations made for dropping our mail after the initial landing. I counted letters as I went to sleep.

In the morning I checked with the Adjutant again, and no cancellation had come in during the night. Maybe the General was serious about this. The advance party truck had already left for the airport. At nine o'clock I boarded the truck detailed for me and moved off with the entire convoy.

When we reached the aerodrome our truck drove up to the plane that was allotted to us. Here I met the pilot who was to fly us in. He was a major from Michigan.

"I'll be taking you in about seven hundred," he said, "and I'll give you the green light about six hundred and fifty. You should all be out at four hundred feet." Then he added, "I've been on lots of drops before, and I haven't missed my target yet." He touched his head with both hands and smiled. We liked this American pilot, and knew that we need not worry.

We fitted on our statachutes, and checked over our equipment, and then lay around on the grass. Photographers were taking photographs, and the American ground crews were asking us all sorts of questions. It all seemed like a football game before the kick-off.

Our pilot came back. "The fighters have just returned. They say there is not much flak to worry us."

The second pilot was warming up the motors of the Dakota. It was 1130 when we boarded the plane. The ladder was withdrawn, and our plane taxied slowly at first across the runway, and then gathered speed. Each man hooked up his static-line, and then swallowed specially prepared tablets which bolstered morale. We felt suddenly a gentle smoothness and knew that we were now airborne. The English countryside lay quiet and indifferent to our fate.

There were hundreds of planes in the air, and all were heading south-east towards the sea. Below was England, spread out as we had seen it many times before. Yet today, it had a special beauty to it, a thrilling sort of suddenness which most of us had never experienced before. Each man thought of what was most sacred to him, and what was happening on the ground below.

No one spoke of anything very serious. Everybody was telling poor jokes. In our plane some of the people were ridiculously happy, and continued to tell stories to one another. One man on my right, who was visibly frightened a minute ago, could not stop laughing. Perhaps the tablets were beginning to take effect, I thought.

Every now and then the American engineer of the Dakota kept coming out of the pilot's cabin to give us the OK sign. The longer we flew, the more often he kept coming out of his cabin to assure us that everything was all right. When I looked out of the door now I could see a few fighter planes darting over the Channel's blue water. I leaned down and strapped my kit bag on to my leg and checked the quick release. Everything seemed to be working. To each side bobbing about us were the other transports.

Presently I was nudged. Below was the low flooded land of Holland. This was no normal venture. It was a leap into the unknown, into a clean, tidy land divided out as squarely as sugar cubes. A little anti-aircraft fire started to blossom around some of the planes. The red light went on. Fifteen minutes before the jump. Every man let his fingers run around his harness, tugging, feeling, and glancing at his static line. I checked the seventy-pound kit bag strapped to my leg again. It looked secure. I could see below me the first railway track. The next railway track we crossed would bring us very close to our dropping zone. The only difference in this countryside to England seemed to be that the houses here were a little squarer.

The physical tension in the plane was beginning to mount. Above us our own fighters were weaving a protective pattern in the sky. Occasionally they would dart down below to strafe an enemy strongpoint.

Unexpectedly the plane began to lose altitude, and to the right of the door I watched the red light. Everybody was standing up in their order of jump. Below me I saw the long ribbon of railway track and knew that our dropping zone would be reached in a minute. Then the red light changed to green. Lieutenant Sutton, who was the first to go, gave a wild shout and was out of the door into space. It was my turn. My kit bag broke loose from my leg. I grabbed it in my arms and stepped out of the doorway. The slipstream carried me away. Then I was tumbling down, down into nothing. Suddenly there was a tug and the tumbling stopped. I was floating gently with a huge blue canopy, as blue as the sky, stretching silkenly above. I looked down in time to see all my belongings scatter as the kit bag burst upon the ground two hundred feet below. Fortunately I had my revolver and tommy-gun with me; also some spare ammunition and grenades.

I was drifting into a small clump of trees and began to pull on my stroud-lines in order to avoid them. I landed in a clearing in the bush, easily, and on my feet. I saw Watts, my batman, who was to join me, hanging from a tree nearby. I threw up my knife. He cut himself loose and crashed down through the branches unhurt. I looked around and orientated myself.

North of us was a big Dutch highway which ran from Amersfoort to Arnhem. Watts and I were to reach this road and gather German transport any way we could.

It was unbelievably quiet on this Sunday afternoon of September 17th. Occasionally we would hear a lone rifle shot. But there was not any real German resistance anywhere. We headed for the open field where our gliders had already landed. Our troops were working furiously to unload all the supplies and vehicles. We crossed the field and followed a little dirt track which branched out to a dirt road. Here I met a paratroop corporal, who was lost and had nothing to do, so he joined us. A little farther down the road we came to a beautiful summer resort hotel, hidden in a growth of woods. It was called the Wolfhezen Hotel. Several Dutch people rushed out and shouted greetings at us, and pointed excitedly to the side of the hotel. There were about twenty meek and defeated Germans with their hands above their heads who came out from around the side of the building and started to empty their pockets of everything they had. For a moment we ignored the Germans. The son of the hotel manager spoke English, and he told us that these Germans had been garrisoned here but there were many more who fled to the north.

Up the road at this time came one of the other Canadian officers who was attached to one of the British Gliderborne Regiments. This was Scotty MacDonald. We exchanged greetings and information, and I handed the prisoners over to him. Then he went up the road looking for one of his gliders which had crashed in the woods. (During the time I was at Arnhem I never saw Scotty again, but later learned that he had been taken prisoner. Since this time he has been repatriated, and is now back in Canada.)

It was much too nice an afternoon to worry about things like war, so we gave one of the Dutchmen a rifle and told him to stand guard at the front of the hotel while we went in to have tea. It was very peculiar having tea in a Dutch hotel in central Holland, with the finest Dutch china, when only two hours ago we had had a mug of tea at an American aerodrome in England. We promised the Dutch family that if we could, we would return that evening to celebrate their liberation with some champagne they had specially hidden for this occasion.

After tea we set out up the dirt road, crossed the railway line and knew we were within a few hundred yards of the double-lane highway. There was a motorcycle lying beside the road, which started after several attempts. We all climbed on and proceeded down the road. A hundred yards ahead we could see the highway. I could not stop the motorbike, and tried to turn around quickly, and the three of us went tumbling off the machine into the bushes beside the road. "Gor Blimey!" said Watts. And he jumped over to the motorbike and turned off the racing motor.

Nearby we heard a groan and turned about quickly. A few yards down the road, in a little clearing beside some bushes, lay a young, blond German lieutenant. He kept crying for water, but we dared not give him any for his stomach had a bullet in it. He was very frightened and his blue eyes were wide and staring with fear. I left the Corporal with him and crept through the bushes to the edge of the paved highway with Watts.

We saw an ambulance standing in the middle of the road, untouched. A little farther down the road was a German touring car resting on its roof with many bullet holes in it. Beside the car, lying twisted and ugly in death, was the German SS driver. This is where the Lieutenant had come from, I thought. Watts whispered that there was a German Red Cross man lying wounded close by. We crept over to have a look at him, and discovered he only had a light wound in the foot, which prevented him from walking. Watts went through his pack and produced two bottles of cognac and a fancy-dress dagger which he put in his smock. Since I needed a pack, I took the rucksack from the German and threw away what I didn't need. The German kept complaining that he needed the cognac for his morale. We let him sniff it, told him not to move, and left to examine the ambulance on the road.

A paratroop sergeant from the Army Service Corps came strolling down the road toward me. It was his job to recover vehicles and we gave the ambulance to him. In a minute he had it started and drove away down the road in the direction from which he had come.

We returned to the young German Lieutenant, and saw the Corporal still sitting beside him smoking enormous German cigars which he had taken out of the German officer's kit bag. He told me that he had just seen one of our jeeps and had told the driver to send up stretcher-bearers to collect the two Germans.

The SS Lieutenant was a typical young Nazi. I watched his eyes wince with the pain from his wounds. He was badly hit, and I knew that he would not live very long. When a man is about to die he assumes the qualities of a normal human being.

And although we knew the record of the German SS, the Corporal had treated this Lieutenant in the same manner he would any of our own men and made him as comfortable as he could in his last few minutes of life. The German Lieutenant died alone and in great fear. We left him and picked up our motorcycle again.

We pushed the machine much more than we rode it, and finally in utter contempt for it we threw it in a ditch. Then we sat down beside the road and had supper. As we were eating, a Dutch policeman with his best girl strolled up to us. He was happy, he said, to be liberated, and made a sign across his neck whenever he spoke about the Germans. On his arm he wore the orange armband which was the sign of the Dutch Resistance. After a brief visit he strolled down the road again with his girl.

It was beginning to get dark, and I decided that I would try to rejoin my battalion as soon as I could. Most of the troops must have moved off long ago in the direction of the high ground which we were to occupy north of Arnhem. When we reached the railway track again we discovered one of our sentries there, and he told us that at Brigade Headquarters we could obtain information as to the location of my battalion.

I told the Corporal to remain beside the railway track and Watts and myself would go down the road to Brigade and find out what we could. We passed the hulls of several crashed gliders beside the road, and, after walking for about twenty minutes, we were challenged by a sentry. I replied with the password and entered Brigade Headquarters. Here the Brigadier told me that my battalion was marching tonight on Arnhem, and that they had been held up by machine-gun fire on the outskirts. Casualties had been heavy. We would not be able to catch up with them tonight. Outside the Brigadier's tent

I saw the stretchers being brought in to the dressing-station across the way. I spoke to the doctor, who told me that he was already a little short of sulpha drugs and penicillin. This was the first omen we had of how the battle was to go. I could hear the distinctive bursts of German machine-guns nearby, and could see streaks of tracer going through the dark. Outside it was already night.

At the railway track I met the Corporal, and together the three of us went back to the Wolfhezen Hotel. Our friends were very happy to see us. They brought out the champagne and the most delectable Dutch foods. After we had eaten we discussed in a mixture of broken Dutch and broken English the great happiness of this occasion. Then they led us upstairs to the guest rooms, and we went to sleep on their best feather beds.

At four o'clock in the morning of September 18th I was awakened. Somebody was shaking me. It was the young daughter of the hotel manager. "Deutches, Deutches," she said. I rose quickly and dressed. Watts and the Corporal were waiting for me downstairs in the kitchen. The family was gathered around the table and they looked at me questioningly, not wanting to believe that their liberation was to go so soon. The young son held the hand of his fiancée and stared at me. The mother and father gathered the two babies in their arms, and their eyes seemed to say, "Don't let the Germans come back now." The noise of machine-guns was filling the dark morning.

Evidently the daughter, who slept downstairs, had seen Germans passing the window of her bedroom, and fearing that we might be caught, had awakened us. We thanked the people for their kindness, and left behind some English silver for the children. The old man went out of the back door to see if the road was clear. He came back to say that he could see nobody. As I went through the door I could hear the mother sobbing softly. We were the last Allied troops they were to see for nine months, until the main army came up from the south to stay.

It was very noisy outside. When we reached the railway line we discovered that the sentry had left. I decided to stay here in the woods until the first light of morning; it seemed an interminable wait.

At eight o'clock in the morning we left the covering of the woods and met a jeep which was speeding along the railway track road and going east. The Lieutenant driving the jeep had been separated from his own regiment during the night. He offered to take us to Divisional Headquarters which was several miles from here. Division was scheduled to move this morning. We jumped into the jeep.

When we arrived at Division I was told by the Major of the operations branch that my battalion was a good distance from here and that I was to remain with Division that morning, as there would probably be a job for me. What the job would be, I did not know.

The Corporal left me here to join his own group, and Watts and myself moved with the division that morning east into the peaceful little town of Oosterbeek. Oosterbeek was only four miles from Arnhem. Evidently we had moved into a residential suburb consisting of very modern and luxurious houses. In the distance we could hear the sporadic burst of machine-gun fire on the outskirts of Arnhem itself. And I knew that this meant that my battalion was trying to secure the approaches to the main bridge across the Rhine.

Along the main Oosterbeek-Arnhem road our convoy stopped for breakfast. I was invited to wash in one of the big white-walled houses. The people were very pleasant to us, and an amazing number spoke English.

The sun was shining and the morning was fine and crisp and invigorating. Today was September 18th, the day the other paratroop brigade of our division was to drop.

The road we were on was well paved, and ran half a mile north of the Rhine and parallel with it. On the south side of the road were the prim Dutch houses of this district which ran into the suburban district of Arnhem. Spaced along the sidewalk were our Bren-gun carriers, jeeps, anti-tank guns and small groups of glider pilots and paratroops who were advancing with the column into Arnhem.

I was sunning myself in a deckchair in the front yard of a house and Watts was trying to find some cans of Spam, when unexpectedly we heard a distant hum of aircraft. These, we thought at first, would be our planes coming to support our drive on Arnhem. The planes were coming out of the sun and looked like streaks of silver, and possibly a little like Spitfires. Then we saw the markings on the wings. They wore black crosses which stood out plainly. Three times the fifteen Messerschmitts dipped their silver noses and strafed small pockets of our troops to the east near the bridge. And as quickly as they had come, they disappeared again. And the last I saw of them they were heading eastward toward Germany. We had been spared the strafing.

Suddenly I heard someone calling my name. The Major, who was second-in-command of Operations, came running over to me.

"I have a job for you; come with me quickly."

He took me across the road to where a jeep was waiting, and said, "There is food and ammunition on the jeep. You've got a radio set, a wireless operator, and a driver. You must try to get through to the bridge. Our last contact with them was early this morning, and at that time they had run out of food, and had very little ammunition left. When you reach the bridge contact us by wireless." He handed me maps and gave me as much information as he could about the road ahead. Then he handed me a bullet-proof vest saying, "You will need this more than I will."

He asked my name and then left me alone with the wireless operator, jeep driver, Watts, and a jeep piled high with provisions.

I went across the road to the house where I had washed that morning. There was a middle-aged Dutchman here who spoke English very well. He was anxious to help us in any way he could. Since he knew this district well, he was the ideal man to be our guide. I asked him if he would.

He asked me to pardon him for a moment. Then he went into the house, and reappeared in a few minutes. On his head now he wore a 1914 Dutch helmet, and around his left arm he wore a big yellow armband with the word "Oranje" on it. I gave him a tommy-gun and told him all he had to do was to press the trigger. Then I gave him the bullet-proof vest, and our little party was ready. I was later to discover that I could not have asked for a better man than this tall, gaunt Dutchman whose name I never learned.[1]

The Major on the Operations staff came running over to me again and gave me another bullet-proof vest. We were an odd-looking expedition. The radio operator sat in the back upon cases of ammunition and food, with his wireless set. Beside him, perched even higher, was Watts on the spare tyre. In the front sat the driver, whose name was Martin, myself on a box of compo rations, and the Dutchman in his plus-fours, tweed

---

[1] It has come to light that this Dutchman was Anthony Knipping.

coat, 1914 helmet, and bullet-proof vest. I looked at my map and we set off down the main road, and soon left behind us our column which was parked alongside the trees. After we had gone about a mile I stopped near a railway bridge and went into a house beside the road. Here I met a major who was responsible for holding this area. He told me that as yet no troops had managed to reinforce the few who were holding the bridge in Arnhem. I told him that my job was to go through to the bridge. He laughed and said that it was impossible.

Ahead of me on the road, the Germans, from the high ground on the left, were occasionally spraying us with machine-gun fire. If I was to go through, it must be a quick, mad dash, I thought, and the quicker the better. Beyond the railway bridge I knew I would find our paratroops in position. I returned to the jeep.

We started on our way again and went underneath the railway bridge and entered the outskirts of Arnhem. As we sped down the road a paratrooper waved frantically for us to pull up. We turned off in the protection of a driveway between two houses.

Here I met Lt.-Colonel Dobie, the Commander of my paratroop battalion. He warned me against trying to get down the road, as his forward company was held up only fifty yards ahead. The battle was going badly. Colonel Dobie had most of his officers either killed or wounded that morning by the heavy calibre machine-gun fire which came down from the high ground to the north.

I decided to leave the jeep here for the time being and go forward on foot to make a reconnaissance. Possibly there would be other ways through.

The most forward position was a house on the right side of the road. Here I met an artillery observer, who told me that the way ahead was impossible. Only if you sped quickly through at night was there a possibility of reaching the bridge. Then my eyes swept south down the slope to my right, where the river Rhine ran. It was only three hundred yards to the river. I saw barges moored to the bank. The river might take us through. I decided I would have a closer look at it and see what it could offer.

When I returned to the jeep I could only find the Dutchman and the radio operator. The three of us went a short distance back down the road and turned off on a little dirt path which wiggled its way toward the river. The river was not visible itself until you came close to it, because in the early fall it is shallow and sunk deeply between the banks. We parked the jeep in some trees and walked carefully the last hundred yards. I heard something whine past my head, and presently the whines began to come more often. The ground was being clawed out around us by a machine-gun sniper. For one hour we dared not move from the shallow ditch where we lay. Each movement brought bullets whining to within inches of us. We were pinned to the ground. We could not use this area now. The Germans would be aware of our interest in the river.

We decided to make a dash for the jeep. In a minute we had it started and were on our way up the winding path to the road. The machine-gun opened up again, but it was too late, for we had already gained the cover of a small embankment. When I reached the main road I had come to a decision. I would try to dash down this road which led to the bridge. I pressed the accelerator until I could press it no more. The jeep leaped ahead past our forward positions. And here is where Fate stepped in. Just as we passed the most forward position, the steering wheel of the jeep came loose, and the jeep careened to the side of the road into the embankment. For a moment the jeep hung on one wheel, swaying as if it would turn over. But on one wheel it stayed. Then about ten yards ahead of us a terrible stream of machine-gun bullets ricocheted and bounced off the road for the next few minutes. If the jeep had gone on, it would have arrived at that position just in time to be riddled. It would have been impossible for anything to have lived on that stretch of road.

The wireless and most of the supplies were scattered in the ditch. The Dutchman had a deep gash on his leg, and the operator and I were a little shaken. We gathered up our supplies and placed them by the ditch, and then rested in the shade. At the moment everything seemed hopeless. We sat and rested here for an hour. Presently from a little side road nearby a Bren-gun carrier slowly approached. I stopped it and saw that the driver was alone. He had deposited some ammunition with the forward troops and was now heading back to Division. We transferred our supplies to the carrier and convinced the driver to have another attempt at the bridge with us. He spat in the dust, gave us a little wink and turned the carrier around. Now its nose pointed toward the bridge.

By this time Martin, our driver, had rejoined us, but Watts was nowhere to be found. And this mild little fellow disappeared forever out of my life. Also, the radio operator had managed to salvage enough of the spare parts to make his set operate. The Dutchman had bandaged his leg and was feeling fine.

We mounted the carrier and turned off a little road to the left, which ran in among the houses of Arnhem. The Dutchman directed the carrier farther and farther east. Now we were almost approaching the heart of Arnhem itself and still we saw no human beings.

Telegraph lines lay on the streets. Telephone poles had been knocked down, and many of the houses around us were smoking and burning. All the buildings in the district were shattered. Shells were bursting everywhere now. We could see the flashes coming from the guns of German tanks which were not more than two hundred yards down the road. The outlines of the German tanks were obscured by the thick pall of smoke which hung over everything. We turned down a driveway between two large houses and stopped.

In one of these houses I could see a few of our own troops moving about. A lieutenant came out from one and asked me if I was a Canadian officer. I said, "Yes." He asked me to follow him toward the house. He directed me towards the back steps, and in order to mount the steps I had to step over the dead body of a major. Then General Urquhart came out, as cool and collected as if he had been to afternoon tea. He greeted me cheerfully and told me he had been out for a day, and wanted to know how I came through. I told him. He gave me several important messages concerning further orders for his troops in the battle, and told me I was to take them back to Divisional Headquarters as soon as possible. He said I was not to go any farther toward the bridge through Arnhem, but if I liked could try my alternative route by the river.

We tried to get through to Divisional Headquarters on the wireless set, but it wouldn't work. I saw a brigadier beckoning the General to follow him into the woods behind the house. He had a small group of men with him for protection, and seemed impatient to move. The General waved goodbye to me, and was gone. We were left alone in the middle of Arnhem.

I decided to stay here and have something to eat. In a moment we were joined by another carrier which whirled into the driveway and stopped beside ours. There were five men on it, and two were badly wounded, one in the eyes, and the other in the shoulder. There was a lieutenant in it who had come to join some of his men in a house which, he said, was several doors away.

"Bloody, filthy battle!" he said. "And it is only the second day." He left me and disappeared into the house next door.

There was a great deal of noise everywhere, but no shells were landing near us. I heard the clanking of enemy tanks not far behind the house and could hear frantic shouts in German. I decided to move.

The first thing to be done was to leave the wounded somewhere where there were kind Dutch people to look after them. The Dutch guide said he knew of a place not far away. With the carrier carrying the wounded following closely behind, we darted out of the driveway and crossed the road strewn with cables and chunks of metal shrapnel, to the protection of a side road nearby. We were heading west now, and in a few minutes stopped at a big white house with a Red Cross flag on it. It was a Dutch hospital. One carrier stopped outside the front and the other went into the driveway at the rear. Guards were posted and we went into the house with the Dutchman.

There were two nurses inside, and at least twenty men, women, and children who were very frightened and hiding in the cellar. When we entered they came up to greet us, but they could not smile. They relieved us of the wounded and gently attended to them. The man with the wound in his eyes cried out that he didn't want to be left alone. The other soldier was now unconscious and very weak from the loss of much blood. We left behind food, and assured the soldier with the bandaged eyes that he would be found here by our own stretcher-bearers in a day or two. It was impossible and dangerous to carry the wounded with us.

I saw the wireless operator take a Bren gun and fire into the top storey of a house close at hand. Then each one of us fired a burst into the house where a German had been seen at the window. If there were Germans there, they were not there now.

We were endangering everyone's life by staying here. Our two carriers moved off on to the road where we had our fated jeep accident. I met some of our rear troops coming up — if one could call them rear troops. They had the transport from the gliders with them. But they had no orders or any place to go. The lines of communication had been cut by the Germans in several places. Many of our troops were lost and wandering. The Germans had infiltrated behind us. And as we advanced, they closed in. They seemed to be everywhere.

I spoke to the transport officer, who later won the D.S.O. for leading the remnants of the battalion out safely on the night of the evacuation. He told me that between here and Divisional Headquarters at Oosterbeek there were none of our troops. The transport officer told me he would bivouac here for the night and wait for orders. I left him with my two Bren-gun carriers and stopped at the little path where I had made my reconnaissance earlier in the day to the river. It was twilight now, and I decided to try and reach the river to inspect the barges again. But first I would wait until it was a little darker. In five minutes the light was just right, and the carriers headed down the path. As soon as we began to descend the slope, a concentration of fire opened up on us. We deployed and fired back. The fire came from German armoured cars patrolling the river bank where we were this afternoon. For half an hour we engaged them in a running battle on the meadows which ran down to the river. The Germans were guarding the barges. They must have expected us to try and use them.

We had no casualties when we retired, but had silenced one enemy machine-gun post. Night had almost fallen as we turned down the main road which we hoped would lead us to Divisional Headquarters.

As we approached the railway bridge, we turned right and stopped at the railway station. I met our transport officer again. He told me that the other paratroop brigade, which had landed this afternoon, had suffered heavily on the dropping from increased anti-aircraft fire. However, the advance elements of the brigade should be passing this way about midnight. Lieutenant Williams had asked me to stay to help in the defence of the transport in case of a German counter-attack during the night. I decided that our little group would stay for several hours until the defence was organized.

During the night the Germans drew closer to the roads and came down from the high ground on the north. They set up their Spandaus and fired on fixed lines at various points across the road which ran from Oosterbeek to Arnhem.

It was just after midnight when the Intelligence sergeant from my battalion came and shook me by the shoulder. I was dozing against a tree.

"Orders, sir, all transport and men to follow me immediately. The situation is serious."

I gave one of my carriers to the Intelligence sergeant, and kept one for myself. The vehicles were already lining up and preparing to follow the Intelligence sergeant back into Arnhem.

With an American officer, who was also trying to get through to Division, I started off. I now had with me a sergeant who drove the carrier, a wireless operator, Martin the jeep driver, and the American wireless Lieutenant. As we passed under the bridge and went down the road I saw troops in single file marching towards me. At the head of the column was a major, behind him was part of the paratroop brigade which had dropped that afternoon. The Major was moving down the road with the purpose of reaching the bridge at Arnhem tonight. I told him as much about the situation ahead as I knew, and he in turn told me where Divisional Headquarters was now located, and then went on. We were to turn right at the second church steeple in Oosterbeek. There was no moon, and the rattling of our carrier down the dark road sounded like a tank. On the high ground the Germans were firing tracers wildly into the sky.

When we turned right at the church steeple, I saw a big building with a small light burning inside, and decided to inquire here. This was a temporary hospital, and inside the rooms were overcrowded with our wounded. The Dutch nurses and doctors were helping our own doctors, and were risking a life in a concentration camp for assisting us. Everywhere there was the stiff smell of antiseptic. No one paid any attention to us; they were much too busy.

I stopped an English doctor who told me that Division was down the road on the left. I thanked him and stepped back out into the night. I did not know we had so many casualties.

When I arrived at Division, I saw the Major who had sent me off to the bridge that morning. I told him that I had arrived within a quarter of a mile of it and had been redirected here by General Urquhart. I told him the message the General had given me. He took me to see the Brigadier who was acting divisional commander, and I related the events of the day to him. Everyone seemed content.

I was then told that I must return immediately to inform the commanders of the three parachute battalions that they were to attack Arnhem bridge that night. The attack had been cancelled, and, since radio communication had broken down, I was to go through by jeep with the message that the attack must go in at once.

I went outside and saw that the driver of the carrier was sleeping. I didn't bother waking him up and thanking him, but transferred the essential supplies to the waiting jeep. With Martin at the wheel, the radio man and the indomitable Dutchman in back, we started off again.

The trip back was uneventful, except for the occasional Dutchman who stood outside his house in a nightgown to give us a little cheer as we passed. After inquiring in the dark, I found the house where the "O" group was being held, rushed in and delivered my message to three colonels who were reading a map by candlelight on a small table. They responded quickly. The attack was on again. We would accompany the centre battalion at zero hour.

At 4.30 that morning of September 19th my jeep moved in with the attack. Another parachute battalion was moving past us in the dark. In this battalion was Lloyd Mackenna, the other Canadian paratrooper at Arnhem. I thought I saw him marching down the road with his platoon, but when I went to overtake him, he had disappeared into the confusion of the darkness and the attack. I never saw him again, for he was reported missing that morning in the attack on the bridge.

There were three axes of attack. One was to our left on the high ground, the other to our right on the lowland by the river, and we were to go down the main road on the centre axis. Our battalion began to move slowly by bounds, down the smoothly paved road to the bridge.

It was almost dawn as the German artillery and mortars started to burst among our troops. As it grew lighter I could see the bridge on the river about five hundred yards ahead. The road on my right, which ran very close to the river bank, offered the troops almost no protection. They were exposed to the enemy on the south bank of the river. Suddenly the morning was split and torn with great resounding crashes. The German heavy anti-aircraft guns on the south bank had levelled their guns and were firing over open sights at us. The morning was full of flying chunks of metal and wounded men. Fire came from every conceivable direction.

I lay flattened behind some trees while Martin and the Dutchman crawled under the jeep for protection. We lay like this for half an hour, while the German guns blew up our men on the lower slopes almost at will. I knew that there would be no advance on the bridge today. The four of us made our way back to the jeep and raced like the wind down the main road which led back to Divisional Headquarters.

General Urquhart had returned after narrowly escaping from the Germans. I told him my story, and he told me to relax for the rest of the morning. We all had some breakfast, reloaded our weapons, and went to sleep under the coolness of a big tree. Three Focke-Wulfs, which came to strafe us, only caused us to turn over in our sleep. We were so tired.

When I awoke there was nothing for me to do, and I was informed that I would be asked for when I was needed.

An hour later our Dakotas flew in, dropping our supplies. They did not seem to know where we were. Most of the supplies dropped north in the town of Arnhem or several miles west of our most forward positions. The Dakotas had to penetrate a wall of anti-aircraft fire to come as near as they did, and that day I saw no fewer than twenty aircraft suddenly point their noses toward the ground and burst into flame. Casualties on the supply drop later became so heavy that it was necessary for the Air Force to ask for volunteers to fly into this area. There was no lack of volunteers. The supplies we did receive became very precious to us.

Later on that day I met an American paratroop lieutenant named Johnny Johnson. We decided to work together in the days ahead. Johnny was originally here to direct our fighter support, but yesterday mortars had destroyed all his radar equipment. We struck up a great friendship which was to last all through the days of Arnhem.

That afternoon Johnny, Martin and myself went out on a reconnaissance of the divisional area which was only about a quarter of a mile square. Everywhere the troops had been beating off heavy German counterattacks. Some of the men had not slept for three days.

Orders came around that day which said that Dutchmen, who had volunteered their help, must leave us and return to their homes. The risk of being captured was growing too great, and if they were taken prisoner, the Germans would be certain to shoot them. The Dutchman who had been with me was personally thanked by the General for the good work he had done. And with a sad heart he left us and disappeared into the anonymity from which he had come. I never saw him again. He had a quiet, unknown bravery which he carried with him wherever he went.

Before dark Johnny and I hunted snipers in the nearby woods. We were not very successful, because each time we drew near to where a sniper was, a group of Dutchmen would suddenly dart from out the woods to give us a cheer, and then vanish again. It was a great game to them. However, that night no snipers returned to harass the Headquarters at the Division.

The most mortared place in the world was the small grounds where Divisional Headquarters was located. There was no immunity for either general or private. They suffered the same. Early in the morning of September 20th, the Germans started mortaring on schedule. It was nine o'clock. The mortaring would start at one end of the divisional area and then work back again. There were always heavy casualties from it.

Reports came in that the Germans had shot an eighty-eight millimetre shell through the wall of our hospital, blowing off the arm of a padre. Johnny and I had decided to investigate and find out if the report was true.

When we began to approach the hospital, somebody began to fire at us with a tommy-gun. We could see Germans running in and out of the building. The hospital was certainly in German hands, and it was less than two hundred yards from Divisional Headquarters.

In this Divisional Headquarters every man from the General to the private found it necessary at one time or another to fight the Germans for his life. On each side there were German positions within shouting distance. And it was not unusual for a stray German to infiltrate to within a few yards of the big house where Divisional Headquarters proper was located.

Most of the day we attached ourselves to the remnants of one of the regiments and helped to drive back the occasional German attack.

Later on Johnny and I decided to take a trip down to the river to see if there was any sign of the Second Army coming up from the south. On our way down it was necessary to pass a battered church whose steeple the Germans were continually trying to knock down. Inside we saw a group of very weary, wet and wounded men. These were the remains of the three battalions who had made the attack on the bridge at Arnhem. There could not have been more than two hundred left, and these had escaped by crawling through ditches half-filled with drainage water. Almost everybody was wounded and wet and covered with mud. By looking out of the big shattered church window toward the open field which ran down to the river, you could see the wounded and the dead lying where they had been struck down by mortar and machine-gun fire while trying to escape.

It was a terrible sight in the church. Each man was weary to his bones, and miserable, and most were wounded. Yet they were filled with such great spirit that they could never be defeated. There was only one officer left from my battalion.

This little band of men was commanded by a major named Lonsdale. He was wounded several times in the face, and when asked if he would go to a house close at hand for treatment, he replied, "I have been hit three times, but I'm still good for several more." He smiled through a blood-caked mouth, and told me they were preparing to take up a position around the church. Then my gaze went up to the broken plates of stained glass still left in the windows and out beyond to the sky. The sun seemed a little red with blood.

At the river Johnny and I could see no sign of the Second Army coming to relieve us.

Everywhere we went weary men with beards, manning guns in slit-trenches, would ask us, "When are the tanks coming up from the south?"

As far as we knew the Second Army was over twenty-five miles away.

That afternoon we went tank-hunting for a German Panther, which had been roaring about for a day in a little wood only a few hundred yards away from Division. Every now and then the tank would come to the edge of the wood and fire down the road at our troops. We decided we would try and wound it at least.

That afternoon we approached the area the Panther was lurking in and took up a position a hundred yards away from the wood in some scrub, and waited for the tank to appear. Johnny put a Piat bomb into the recess of the Piat. The clanking and roaring seemed to be coming very close. In a minute the track of the tank could be seen knocking down the trees as it approached the clearing. I steadied the Piat and squeezed the trigger. The recoil knocked me back as the bomb went off, and for a minute the tank was obscured by smoke billowing in front of it. We had hit a track. The German tank began firing wildly and crashed back into the woods again. A few moments later we heard excited German voices. Then silence enveloped the woods.

We returned to Divisional Headquarters and were greeted by Martin, who had prepared for us a delicious supper of sausages, ham, potatoes, stewed apricots, and tea. We then realized that this was the first meal we had eaten in fifteen hours. We lay down beside our jeep and rested.

That night an orderly came looking for me and said I was to report to the General immediately. When I entered the small room which had once been a study, I could see the General at work on several maps of the area, and he had on a pair of earphones. The room was thick and close with cigarette smoke. The General was speaking over the wireless to one of his Brigadiers. Everything he said and did was calm and confident. But he didn't smile now quite as often as he did two days ago. He took off his earphones, laid them wearily down before him, and said, "Would you like to try and get through tonight to the bridge at Arnhem?" He told me that I was under no compulsion to go, and must accept only of my own free will. A few weak signals on the wireless had come through that night from some who still held on. But no one could possibly hold on after tonight. The General would let us have anything we needed for the journey.

I asked for two jeeps filled with supplies, a Dutch guide and an interpreter. We would arrange for the rest ourselves. When I went outside it was dark, and after probing into several slit-trenches I collected two glider pilots, Johnny, and all our personal equipment.

The Dutchman, who was to come with us, spoke English with a heavy Oxford accent. He was Oxford educated and had been loaned from the Dutch Army to the Airborne Division for this operation. His name was Martin Knottenbelt. (Martin, except for a very small part of his life, was bred in England. He had been with the Commandos when they made their raids on German-held France. Later on he went to India where he served with the Commandos again in their terror raids against the Japanese. When Martin escaped from Arnhem he returned to England. From here he was dropped several months later deep behind the German lines in Holland to prepare intelligence and direct the Underground in sabotage until the main forces broke through to him. Martin and I have met many times in England to become close friends, but on this night neither of us expected to see each other again.)

Martin demands well-planned schemes under almost any circumstances. Before I could speak he went outside the house and reappeared with a sleepy-eyed local who carried a tommy-gun and had on an old British uniform and wore a pair of German jackboots.

Then for one hour I gave Martin different plans, and after conferring in Dutch with the local, Martin would discard most of them. Finally I offered a plan which he accepted. By this time Johnny had notified me that he would be sleeping in the corner and to awaken him when there was general agreement.

We were to travel in two jeeps, with a tommy-gunner in the back of each, down to the ferry, which we presumed was still held by our Engineers. The jeeps were to cross on the ferry, and we were to head south until we contacted the tanks from the Guards Armoured Division. We were then to take a tank and clear out the Germans on the south side of the Arnhem Bridge and then take supplies across in the tank.

The plan somehow sounded too easy, but Martin was satisfied.

As we went down to the river that night we passed many men alongside the road. We thought at the time these were our own troops. However, we later discovered they were Germans, but somehow they did not seem interested in us. At the edge of the river we saw no one. The ferry was at least twenty feet from shore. Stretched from the ferry to our bank was a heavy metal cable.

One of the glider pilots who was travelling with us came up to me. He had just seen two members of the engineer party that were supposed to have been in position at the ferry. He told me they had been attacked by the Germans only half an hour ago and had beaten them back with hand grenades.

Someone had to reach the ferry off shore. Since I was in charge of the party, it seemed that I was to do it. Besides, no one else was anxious to get wet; it was too chilly. I told Martin and Johnny to wait for me with the jeeps and that I would try and bring the ferry back to shore. How I was to do it, I did not know.

The cable was sufficiently high above the water so that if I crossed my legs over it I could hang with my rear end dipped in the water, and with my hands pull myself along the cable to the deck of the ferry. I grabbed the cable and pulled myself hand over hand to the ferry.

The ferry itself moved across the river by means of the cable which reached from one bank to the other. If you wound a big iron wheel on the ferry, it would take up the steel cable and pull you into shore. If you let the wheel go, it would unwind itself and the ferry would go out into the stream again. And if, when the wheel unwound, you would begin to wind it again in the reverse direction, you could pull yourself across the river the opposite way. The iron wheel was stopped from unwinding by a lever. I removed the lever and before I could stop the wheel from unwinding, the ferry slipped out into the stream another twenty feet from shore. It was impossible to wind the wheel myself. I needed the help of another man. The night was very dark. There was no moon out and there was a heavy mist in the air. I could barely see the shore. I shouted for Johnny to come out. In a few minutes he was with me. Together we tried to turn the wheel. We could not move it. We then discovered by examining the mechanism that the gears had been smashed by the Germans. We had no other choice but to return to the bank.

When the two of us reached shore our clothes were sopping wet. The cable by now was well under water, and to bring ourselves back we found it necessary to almost swim. We could not possibly cross the river that night by ferry.

On our way back to Division we made enough noise to resemble a tank regiment on the move. Martin honked his horn several times. I turned on two brilliant headlamps by accident. We heard scurrying and running in the bushes to either side of the road. We had frightened the Germans away.

When we reached Division the Dutch guide, Martin, and the two glider pilots disappeared back into the night. During the rest of my time with the First Airborne Division at Arnhem I never saw any of these people again.

Johnny gave me a pair of his extra pants and, disregarding the shelling, the two of us went to sleep in the top floor of the house that was Divisional Headquarters.

At nine o'clock next morning we were punctually awakened by a cascade of mortar shells which were landing almost every second. The mortars rained down incessantly.

We got dressed and went downstairs. The calendar had September 21 marked with a circle. This was the fifth day, and we were supposed to hold out at the most for only forty-eight hours. No one seemed to know where the Second Army was, but the Operations branch seemed confident they were only a short distance from us. Tonight their forward elements should reach the southern bank of the river.

I reported to Colonel Preston, in charge of Operations, and he told me to go around with my two jeeps, which by now had become known as "The Flying Patrol", and shoot up small parties of Germans who had infiltrated into the woods around us. All I could find was one jeep with our driver Martin. Johnny in the meantime had managed to pick up some spare grenades, a box of compo rations, and several additional Bren guns. The mortaring was very heavy now. The Germans had the area ranged perfectly, and almost everyone at Division was suffering from some sort of mortar wound. We decided to get away from here quickly.

We reached the perimeter where our forward elements were living in houses in Oosterbeek. I noticed that the faces of the men had become very gaunt. They were all very tired. And in their eyes you could see that they were grieving and ailing, but they never complained. They only asked, "When are the troops going to be here from the south? Do you think it will be tonight?" We cheered them up by telling them that the Polish Paratroops were dropping on the south bank of the river that afternoon, and that we were to have a huge supply drop also.

All that afternoon and morning we chased Germans out of houses, shot up snipers, and gave our help to troops who needed additional fire power.

In the afternoon we saw the Dakota fleet come in from the west to drop the Polish paratroopers. Lines of German tracer bullets went up into the sky to meet them. Some of the planes began to wobble evasively to avoid the anti-aircraft fire, but none were hit. Then in sticks of eighteen the men came out of the doors and floated earthward. One Brigade had dropped on the south bank successfully.

A few minutes later the Dakotas with our supplies appeared from the north. Most of them never really had a chance to reach us. At least fifteen aircraft were shot down. As they were hit they would burst into flame and arc toward the earth. Those that reached a place anywhere near our area quickly jettisoned their supplies. We received very little resupply that day. Everybody helped to bring in the dropped containers to our concentration area.

Later on we drove our jeep into the garage of a little house in Oosterbeek which was partially hidden by trees from the estates of two larger houses on each side of it. We often used this little garage to cook a meal in when we wanted to get away from the shelling and mortaring. The houses around appeared deserted, and we had never seen any people in this area since we had used this hideout.

As we ate our lunch a young Dutchman visited us. He spoke very good English, and we gave him some of our food.

"You are having a hard time," he said. "And the people are afraid the Germans will come back to Oosterbeek again. Today I saw a German tank just a hundred yards down the road from here. The Germans asked me if I knew where your troops were. But of course I did not tell them. Could I be of help in any way to you?"

I thanked him and assured him that soon our tanks would cross the river and there would be no doubt about which way the battle would go.

After lunch we visited another Dutch house. Inside was an aged Dutch couple. They told us their daughter was in Montreal. The old lady knew exactly what our plight was as she listened daily to both the German and English newscasts. If we ever had to hide, she told us, we could use her house.

We stayed most of the afternoon in the garage. The Germans were using a loudspeaker. They were imploring us to surrender because we were hopelessly outnumbered and had no chance of survival. Then they would broadcast a long list of the prisoners they had taken, and the names of our dead. They said that out of our original force of eight thousand, there were only three thousand left fighting. They knew a great deal about us, and we grew angry because we knew they were right. Then they assailed us with swing music. It certainly was funny. Here we were in the middle of Holland and surrounded by Germans, listening to this music.

Johnny and I decided that night to cross the Rhine and contact our forces coming up from Nijmegen. Martin, the driver, was to wait here for us with the jeep for thirty-six hours. If we were not back by then, he was to return to Divisional Headquarters. We stripped ourselves of all excess equipment and started out for our troops, dug in a few hundred yards from the river edge.

When we reached them, we discovered they were the remnants of a machine-gun company. They had heavy casualties, and the dead and the living shared the same slit-trenches. We warned them that three of us would be going down to the river that night at dusk and that our signal for returning was to be two white dashes given by our flashlight. The third member of our party was a Dutch-Englishman in the Commandos who was to come along as our interpreter. His name was Goebitz.

At dusk we left the forward slit-trenches. The men wished us good luck as we crawled by them into the field ahead. We had to cross over an open, unprotected field two hundred yards long, but it was very dark and no one saw us. We reached the hedge, which was only fifty yards from the river. We looked through a slit in the hedge and saw the way ahead of us clear. We went through and crawled to a stone promontory which jutted out into the swift river current. The south bank looked only fifty yards away, but we knew it was over two hundred and fifty yards across. We inflated the life preservers we had brought with us and tied them together to form a raft. Just as we were preparing to strip and enter the water, we heard the sound of paddles and men's voices, in a language we did not understand. I moved fifty yards downstream and saw troops coming across in rubber dinghies. They were the Polish Paratroops. Johnny was with me.

I asked the Polish officer to tell Goebitz we were going to cross, and have Goebitz show him the way to Division. The Polish officer said he understood. (Goebitz was never told and waited by the river until he was taken prisoner.) Johnny and I and two Poles boarded the dinghy, and in five minutes we were across the Rhine. Then began the job of pulling the rubber dinghy across fields, hills and over fences until the Poles beckoned us to be cautious. They indulged in an unintelligible conversation with each other for several moments, then one gave a short grunt. It was answered by another short grunt, and the four of us crossed over a knoll and saw about a hundred Poles congregated around a figure speaking English in the centre. It was Lt.-Col. Meyers, D.S.O., the engineer officer from Division. He had crossed the river previously that night and was now trying to ferry the Poles across by rubber dinghies as quickly as possible to reinforce us.

We told him we were heading south at early morning to contact the tanks coming up, and he wished us luck. That night we discovered a barn filled with luscious Dutch apples. Some we ate and some we slept on.

Very early on the morning of September 22, the Dutchman whose barn we had slept in, brought us some brown bread and milk. We thanked him. Then Johnny and I moved off south through the apple orchards, avoiding the roads where we had seen some Germans walking around earlier that morning.

We saw a "duck" (an amphibious truck) overturned and loaded with supplies in a ditch, but we saw no troops. After moving south another mile we could see a column of tanks and transport with infantry moving about five hundred yards away. Our first thought was that they were Germans. We waited and watched. We decided that they were our own troops and advanced cautiously along a little road toward them.

After we had gone a hundred yards we noticed the brown mushroom hats of the British Tommy mingling with the grass above a hastily-dug slit-trench. The Tommies recognized us and we passed through. We also passed through a squadron of Sherman tanks and many amphibious vehicles until we finally reached the Headquarters of the leading infantry battalion. I told the Colonel the seriousness of the situation, and I then repeated to the Brigadier in charge the same thing. That night I was instructed there would be an effort to get the remainder of the Polish Paratroops across to reinforce us. (It never materialized. The Poles were squandered away without effect.)

After we arrived Johnny and I were fed and then we went to sleep for most of the afternoon. When we awoke the Lt.-Colonel of the British Fourth Dorset battalion asked me to point out to him, the best way I could, our approximate positions on the far bank of the river. As we walked toward the river bank we could see the Dakotas coming in with their supplies. Once again the performance of yesterday was repeated. All but a very small proportion of the supplies were dropped to the Germans; the rest landed in the vicinity of our Divisional Headquarters. Many of the Dakotas crashed that day, because the anti-aircraft fire was very intense and very accurate.

When I returned with the British Lt.-Colonel to his Battalion Headquarters, I met a British paratrooper who had escaped from the bridge by swimming the river. He told me that the last of our paratroopers had left the bridge three days ago; so even if I had got through, there would have been no one to supply. The temptation now was too much, however, and I decided that afternoon to make a quick trip by jeep to the bridge and see what I could.

There was no difficulty in getting to within five hundred yards of it, and I studied it through my field glasses. There was considerable German movement, and on the north side I could see German tanks moving about. Then I returned to the British Infantry Battalion and met Johnny.

Johnny had contacted his rear party at Nijmegen earlier in the day and would return there tomorrow. But before he returned he would cross the river tonight with me once again. That night I met the operations officer of our division, a Col. MacKenzie. He had crossed from the north bank also last night, and had contacted Second Army Headquarters, and told them of our precarious position. He told me that the thin road from Nijmegen to the river was all we held, and that German tanks were continually cutting it, making it very dangerous for transport moving up to us.

That night Colonel MacKenzie, Johnny and myself all crossed the river in our rubber dinghy. We hid it in the hedge on the north bank, then parted company with Lt.-Col. MacKenzie and went to see if Martin was still in the garage. The garage was deserted. Martin was nowhere to be seen. We then returned to Divisional Headquarters.

Everybody had by this time moved into the cellar of the house where the wounded were. Tanks had been firing at this house from point-blank range, and mortaring had destroyed most of what was left. The cellar stank with the odour of the gangrenous and the dead. It was awful.

We discovered from Intelligence that the situation had deteriorated considerably. Food and ammunition were running very low. I received permission to return across the river again that night and to help in the assault which the Infantry were to launch from the south bank next day.

That night Johnny and I passed along a narrow path we knew quite well which led to the river. Everywhere in the bushes around us we could hear the Germans moving and talking. We reached our rubber dinghy without trouble, put it in the water and crossed over to the south side.

On the south side of the river British Infantry were billeted in houses near the little town of Elst. We chose the most luxurious house and entered to find a huge, white, downy bed, lying invitingly before us. We both slept in it. In the middle of the night we were shaken awake. A huge Pole was towering above the bed, shaking us. He asked me if we had crossed the river from Arnhem. I said we had. He looked at us, told us we were sleeping in his bed, smiled, and left. This Polish officer had just come from the river where he had attempted to put the Polish Brigade across. The Germans had ranged their heavy guns on the Poles and had blown most of the boats out of the river. This big man, whose bed we occupied, was the Polish General.

We awoke late next morning. It was September 23. Johnny said he must be off to Nijmegen. We shook hands and he was gone. I have not seen him since that time and ten months have already passed by.

That morning I saw the Dorset Infantry Battalion commander, and he told me that at midnight they were definitely to assault across the river, and I would be needed to show them the positions of our airborne troops on the north side.

In the afternoon I met Lt.-Col. Meyers, the Divisional engineer officer, whom Johnny and I had met on the river bank two nights ago. Together we planned, with some R.A.S.C. officers, how we could bring amphibious vehicles loaded with supplies across the river with the Infantry assault.

My job was to go across in one of the leading assault boats and show the Infantry the general direction of the paratroop positions, and then at a given signal, which I was to give with my flashlight, Col. Meyers would despatch the amphibious ducks across the river to me. I in turn was to take the ducks to

Divisional Headquarters. I envisaged trouble. The place the Infantry assault boats were to touch down at was at the ferry landing where we had tried to take our jeeps across three nights ago. The area was too far west of our positions. The Infantry would have much additional work to reinforce us. However, artillery tasks had been prepared with the medium guns and everything was co-ordinated. It would mean delaying the assault another night if we did not attack tonight at midnight.

I saw again that evening the paratrooper who had managed to escape from the bridge at Arnhem two days ago. His name was Fokes. He was a big fellow from Lancashire, and he spoke with a soft Midland accent. He would come with me tonight.

At eleven o'clock we assembled in an orchard which lay behind a high dike. The assault boats were drawn up among the trees. In front of the dike, and at the bottom of twenty feet of grassy slope lay the black, sullen river. I had crossed it so many times during the past two nights that tonight it seemed almost like an old friend. Everything was very quiet except for an occasional mortar crunching nearby. Then a voice said, "Midnight. Let's go."

We grabbed the side of the assault boat, pulled and shoved it over the dike, down the grassy bank and into the water. There were twelve of us. Four men paddled it. In a few minutes we were across to the north shore and touched down at the old ferry road and scrambled ashore. The engineers had already pushed off again and we could see them paddling back to the far bank. The eight of us lay still on the pebbly shore. Fires to both sides of us lit the sky and water with a ghastly yellow glow. A big factory to the left of us was belching flames. Out in the water I could see the ferry; it was almost in the same position as we had left it, except that now it had been sunk, and it jutted a gashed, ugly prow out of the water.

All about us mortars were coming down regularly. And the Germans tried to seal off the river by an almost incessant machine-gun fire. Our boats were blown out of the water by mortars that night, and others, pierced by machine-gun bullets, sunk. The Germans were awake to their danger and were ranging a deadly covering of fire upon the river. The Infantry were having trouble.

A few yards to the right of us another assault boat landed, the last one we were to see that night. The officer crawled toward me. I pointed in the direction of the airborne troops. With a weird shout he scrambled away, and his infantrymen scurried along behind him.

I was turning over in my mind the possibility of going down the road ahead of me with the Ducks. An intermittent stream of fire was coming from the bushes on the right. We could hear the Germans shouting at each other, and pulling logs across the road. It would be mad to signal the Ducks to come across tonight.

We were in a five-yard square of gravel road which sloped down to the river. Each time we slid back down the road to avoid the machine-gun fire, we moved the lower part of our bodies further into the water. We were literally hemmed in by fire. For some reason the Germans thought our major effort was to be at the ferry road, and they concentrated most of their fire on us. There was an Infantry major with me who was calling frantically for Artillery support from the far side of the river. I could hear the voice of the Artillery major on the far bank drift lazily back. "It's all right, old boy. Take it easy. We can't afford to waste any ammunition. But I'll see what we can do." Later on one lone shell crashed into the German positions ahead, and that was all. We were too desperate to become annoyed.

The paratrooper with me was preparing to swim back across the river to our troops. This would be his second escape by swimming the Rhine. Last time he had done it from the bridge in Arnhem. I told him to report to Col. Meyers when he got back and tell him our position. I would stay a little longer and see if things eased up. When I turned around a minute later Fokes was gone. Already he was out in the black waters of the Rhine, swimming strongly for the far bank. I did not relish the idea of a swim tonight.

The fire on our temporary beach-head became more concentrated. It was growing a little light, and it would be suicidal to be caught here in the morning. I stripped off my excess clothing, threw away my tommy-gun, put my revolver in my belt, and slipped into the water. The water was pleasantly warm, and I floated easily out into the stream. I began to swim and realized I was being carried much too far down the river. When I landed on the south bank I knew I was over a mile away from our Infantry bridgehead. For a moment I could not see or hear anyone. I listened in the water. I heard Germans talking low and nervously to each other. It would be easier, I thought, to swim back again to the north bank and wait there until the Infantry had secured a large bridgehead, rather than risk being caught here on the south shore. Surely we would have a bridgehead somewhere on the north side by now. I found a small log, and holding on to it with one hand I pushed out into the river again. This was a mistake. The log carried me swiftly downstream. I passed the raging fires on the north bank, and floated by a huge barge anchored in the river. Then I let go the log and swam with all my energy to a stone promontory which lay foreboding and huge in the dark. I was now on the north shore, about three miles west of the ferry road. This was German territory.

I made my way along the promontory to the grassy slopes of the bank and lay down. To the east great fires were raging in Oosterbeek and Arnhem. The fires and the moon combined to form a myriad of fantastic forms, which shifted about on the changing black river. Sometimes I saw assault boats, sometimes I saw many men swimming, and once I saw a great raft filled with Germans descending upon the Infantry on the far bank.

I was cold and shivering now. I had lost my revolver in the river, and all I had on was a pair of shorts and a battle jacket whose contents the river's bottom had claimed long since. If I did not get up and warm myself, I knew I would contract pneumonia. I still had my watch. It was two o'clock. I had been in the water almost an hour. I began to trot up and down the bank to keep warm, and forgot all about Germans. It was strangely quiet here.

Suddenly in English I heard shouted at me, "Who is that?" The voice had a slight accent. I decided to play along. I went over and met the German in the slit-trench. He pointed his machine-gun at me and began to greet me in very good English. There were two Germans here. One, who was about eighteen, every now and then fired his machine-gun up into the sky to bolster his confidence. The other was about thirty. These people were very nervous. They insisted on shaking my hand. They gave me chocolate, but it was our chocolate. They said they did not want to fight me and were really my brothers. They complied with my every wish. They were very scared.

Later on the older German took me back to his Battle Group Headquarters. I was shivering and shaking in my underwear and was a pitiful and dejected-looking human specimen. The German officers looked at me and the battalion commander gave me his own bed of clean sheets and warm thick blankets. Then a servile little German came around to me seeking intelligence. He was the Intelligence officer and was not particularly successful or intelligent in his interrogation. He was very solicitous and fatherly and tucked me into bed.

I spun the most fantastic yarn I could think up in my present condition. I gave him a wrong name and rank and together we discussed the futility of war and how under the skin we all were brothers. These troops were ordinary Wehrmacht and seemed very gullible. The Intelligence officer went away and brought back dry underclothing, a civilian shirt, a civilian pair of trousers, a pair of stockings and no shoes. He apologized profusely for my lack of comfort, tucked me in again, and left.

The ordinary German soldier, I discovered, had certain almost maternal qualities one could play upon, if one took the correct approach. I was playing upon their vulnerability for all I was worth, and already I had a plan of escape. But first I must get food and shoes. I was very tired, and, in spite of the strange surroundings, I went to sleep.

About eight o'clock next morning a German quartermaster was shaking me awake. He bid me dress and follow him. I walked north down a road for about a mile, which was lined with German Infantry on both sides. Everybody was watching me limp down the road in my stockings, which by now were torn to ribbons by the rough roadbed. The Quartermaster was jabbing his revolver in my back telling me to hurry up. A car came down the road. He shouted to the driver, who stopped. The Quartermaster shouted again and the car turned around and sped down the road with me inside. I was taken out to another headquarters situated in a little town about two miles back from the river. I was given a cup of ersatz coffee and a chair. Presently the Colonel's company commanders entered.

They heiled Hitler and sat down. They were discussing plans upon a map. The map was too far away for me to see.

I was told to follow the Quartermaster again. He took me to another car which travelled in a westerly direction, and after half an hour stopped at a Red Cross station. I went inside and was told I could rest upon the stretcher on the ground. The attendant gave me some cheese and a drink of brandy. I went to sleep. When I awoke I was again moved a few hundred yards down the road to a German reinforcement camp. Here I was put in a tent with half a dozen German soldiers. They gave me some advocaat to drink. It was raining and miserable outside. Everyone was eating our rations and chocolate and smoking our cigarettes from supplies dropped for us. They all tried to be friendly and discover points of similarity with me. One came from America, another had lived in England, someone else had a brother in Canada, and the remainder were fighting the war against their will.

The one who spoke English asked me if we treated our prisoners as well as I had been treated. I assured him we did, but we also gave boots to our prisoners. They said they were sorry but they had none. I offered the only remaining item I had of any value, my watch, for boots. One almost gave me an extra pair of storm boots for it, but he looked around nervously at his companions and said he could not do it. He was frightened they might tell. These Germans knew they were beaten. Their arrogance and self-assuredness had vanished. They were a defeated group of men.

Later on in the day I transferred to another car and was driven away to the little town of Harskamp, where I was put in a barrack room with other British prisoners. I saw some men from the Dorset Infantry Regiment, glider pilots, and some paratroops. I met a glider pilot who seemed anxious to escape.

We discussed various means. The windows were barred, and a young Dutch SS trooper with glasses followed us about continually wherever we walked in the room. We discarded our ideas for the moment. Today was September 25.

In an hour we were moved again by truck to a little village nearby. Here we were installed in a big, vacated German barracks. It was well guarded and Gestapo men in civilian clothes walked continually through the grounds. There were twenty officers and over a hundred other ranks here. We ate one meal a day consisting mainly of potatoes. Fortunately I was not very hungry most of the time. We slept here for the night.

Next day, after much persistent arguing and protestation, I was given a pair of rubber boots. It was what I wanted; they made no noise as I walked and were reasonably comfortable.

Most of the day I lay out in the sun and searched the grounds with my eyes for a weak point in the surroundings. There was no time to plan, however, for we were to walk that night to a little town called Stroe, five miles away from here. In a day we were to leave by train for Germany. That day our party was augmented by several hundred other ranks and a few more officers, all from the paratroops.

That night we marched through a little town, and I saw a great and heartening sight. The Dutch people who lined the sides of the road waved at us when the Germans were not looking. From a top window of a house a lady stood in defiance of the Germans and shouted encouragement down to us. A little boy travelling in a wagon turned around and with two fingers gave a little V sign. Along the route men went to brush a fly away from the side of their face and their hand would be shaped in a V. Spontaneously our little column burst into "There'll Always Be an England", and some of the older men were crying. It was a very touching sight. It did us much good to see how overwhelmingly the Dutch people were on our side, and how deep their feeling toward us was. On the march the guards were two deep on the column sides and whenever we halted they followed us about and took us back to the column again if we strayed.

We reached a big warehouse that night in Stroe. It was situated a hundred yards from the railway junction where we were to board the train for Germany. The officers slept in a small straw-littered room. A much larger portion of the warehouse, adjacent to us, contained the remainder of the troops. On the wall of our room were carved the names of prisoners who had passed through here before us. There were many names on the wall. Some of the men put their own names on the wall with the date they arrived. Today was the 26th of September.

Next morning more officers and men came. I managed to find out what had happened to the First Airborne Division from these new arrivals.

The Dorset Regiment, which had tried to reinforce the Airborne, had been captured, killed or wounded almost to the last man. And last night the order had come for the First Airborne Division to evacuate. The evacuation had been carried out by the Twenty-Third Field Company of Canadian Engineers. All night long their power-driven storm boats plied between the two shores evacuating as many as they could. Their boats were blown out of the water, many men were killed, but still the work went on.

When dawn came many men were left upon the north bank. And the shore had upon it a carpet of dead. These gallant engineers, who evacuated those who still remained after nine terrible days, were the forgotten men in the list of honours. Out of the total of eight thousand airborne troops, only eighteen hundred came back that night to tell their story. This was told to me in our prison camp, and I knew that we were now alone upon the north side of the Rhine, and unlikely to be overtaken by our own troops for some time.

Here in this camp I met Goebitz, the Dutch Commando, whom I had left on the river bank the night Johnny and I met the Poles crossing in their rubber dinghies. He was being treated as a partisan and was in solitary confinement. He had been captured by a German patrol several nights ago and had been shot through the foot.

As I had a pair of civilian pants on, a pair of rubber boots, an old shrunken battle blouse and no hat, I was told by the German commandant that I would probably be considered, when we reached Germany, as an offender against the Geneva Convention. I protested and told him that the clothes had been given to me by the Germans. It seemed to make no difference.

That day I disappeared from the officers' room and mingled with the other ranks. There were too few officers, and since officers were watched more closely than other ranks, I decided to discard my badges of rank to make myself inconspicuous.

I noticed that several Germans, who spoke good English, attempted to befriend some of the troops in order to extract information. The troops took all the cigarettes the Germans offered and told them nothing. Their strategy was very obvious.

Next I found a glider pilot called Kettley and a paratroop sergeant called "Tex" Banwell who were also eager to escape, and we decided at all costs to remain together. All that day we discussed plans for escaping. We were to leave tonight from the siding, only fifty yards away, to board our train for Germany.

Between us we had an escape compass, an escape file, a tin of emergency chocolate, a silk escape map, a box of matches, a blanket, and one cigarette lighter.

That twilight just before we were to leave the camp for the siding, three Spitfires swooped down from the sky and machine-gunned the train. They swooped away as quickly as they had come. Now we could not leave that evening (September 27) for the train engine was destroyed.

All next day we waited for an opportunity to leave the camp to gather wood or collect water, but none came. That night we were lined up outside the big warehouse where we lived. We were counted. There was one officer short. I was very conspicuous in my civilian trousers and was forced to leave Tex and Kettley in the meantime. Then the guards marched us to cattle cars we were to travel in. I marked the cattle car in my mind to which Tex and Kettley were allocated. I followed the guard to the cattle car the officers were to occupy. There were many guards around the twenty-five cars, and the Germans had thrown a cordon around the entire area.

When I reached the car I was to enter I noticed that half of the car was occupied by officers, the other half by German SS troops. The officers were tightly crammed. One of the officers spoke German and said something to the effect that they were so tightly squeezed that it was impossible to have another officer in. The guard hesitated. Then I pointed back to the car that Banwell and Kettley had disappeared into. He took me there and pushed me inside. I shouted to Banwell and Kettley. They were there. And then I heard the door being shut and bolted behind me. The men inside were packed almost body to body, some were wounded and some were not. Most of the men here were from the Dorset Infantry Regiment. They were tired and demoralized.

The cattle car was built on the European style, not being more than twenty-five feet long and not more than seven feet across. Light came in through one small porthole at the front end. I stepped over swearing men and tired men and wounded men, until I was by the window. Kettley took out his file and started to pry at the bottom of the porthole. In five minutes he had the glass out, and there was a round opening left about six inches in diameter. On the outside there were many strands of almost rusted barbed wire. We waited until the train had been going for about five minutes. And then I put both hands around the opening, braced my leg against the side and pulled with all my strength. One rotten board gave way. I pulled again and to our complete amazement a partition about eighteen inches high and three feet wide unhinged from the side. We could ask for no better luck. Kettley commenced to cut the barbed wire strands. I called for Banwell. He came up quickly. In a minute enough wire was cut to allow one man through. I asked if there were any volunteers to go with us. Only one man volunteered, but he was wounded in the leg and it was impossible to take him. The remainder of the Infantry in the car either slept or were so shocked from so many months of fighting that they lacked the will at the moment for the decision.

We could wait no longer. I climbed out and waited at the junction between the two cars until I saw Kettley's head appear. Then I jumped, rolled down the embankment and lay still in the grass. Two more figures jumped out and also lay still in the grass. I waited for what seemed like an interminable length of time until the last coach winked a dark red light back at me. I could hear the German guards singing and talking. And then the train was gone in the night, and there was only silence left.

Presently a figure joined me. It was Kettley and he was soon joined by Tex Banwell. We waited and listened, but no one else came. We decided to march north-west and hoped to return to England by boat if we could reach the Zuider Zee. We took an oath together that night that we would all reach safety and never separate unless the circumstances were very exceptional. I looked up, there were no stars. I took out the compass and we set a course north-west. Kettley and Banwell fell in behind me and we were on our way.

After two hours marching through fields and over sandy, marshy country we reached a great paved highway. It was the main Apeldoorn-Amersfoort road. There was a big convoy of trucks going slowly along the road south-west. We waited by the side and watched the tarpaulin-covered vehicles pass us by. We wondered what we could do if we had a Bren gun with us. When the convoy passed we crept quickly across the road and into the bushes on the other side. All night we kept to the wooded country and small paths, always walking north and west.

In the early morning we stopped in a wood on the outskirts of a tiny village and with our blanket covering us we went to sleep. We had accomplished our first objective and had covered roughly fifteen miles that night.

When we awoke in the morning of September 30th we decided to visit a little cottage. The people were very poor and very friendly and offered us some coffee. We accepted, but soon left them and started off again. A man on a bicycle came up to us. He bade us follow him quickly. He led us to a larger farmhouse and here one of the children was despatched to bring a local member of the Underground back. They fed us here on eggs, milk, butter, coffee, and gave us civilian clothes to wear. They were very kind. Tex was so overcome by his treatment and so grateful that he kissed the old grandmother goodbye. We thanked them, and with the member from the local Underground as our guide we moved off again to another house.

This Underground man was named Osterbek and his wife spoke perfect English. Once again we were fed sumptuously and then taken up to the loft of the barn to sleep. It was late afternoon when we awoke. Mrs. Osterbek told us to come down and follow her. She took us across a field of wheat to another farm where two motorcycles were awaiting us. Mrs. Osterbek gave each of us a silver coin from the time of Philip the Second. She had dug many of these coins up from her garden. They were very valuable. She said it was to remember herself and her family by. Their kindness we could never forget. Tex gave Mrs. Osterbek, as a souvenir, an English pound which he had hidden in an inside pocket.

I got on the back of one motorcycle. Tex and Kettley got on the back of the other, and through narrow, winding back paths we set off. Half an hour later we reached a little chicken coop. Inside I met some of the men who had kept Holland alive through four years of occupation.

One was a tall, blond, professional soldier in golfing pants and a tweed jacket. Two were university professors who wore dirty, blue jeans. The other one I met was a local councilman who was dark and small and kept to himself. These were the men who nightly went about disrupting communications and shooting German transport off the road. If they were caught, they risked a fate worse than death. They were a fine group of men. They showed me the Dutch SS troops they had as prisoners. These were Dutchmen turned traitor who were in the employment of the German Army. They were hooligans and ranked among the cruellest troops I have ever met.

They had received a Bren gun from a plane drop a few days ago and were anxious to be shown how to use it. This Tex did. Another dropping was to take place tomorrow night. They asked us if we would like to try out the Bren gun on German transport that would be moving up the road tonight. We were delighted at the opportunity.

That night a car drove us to a little side road and from here we crept out to the main road and lay still in a ditch. We waited for an hour and presently two heavily laden trucks came lumbering down the road. Tex pulled the trigger. The first truck careened into the ditch. The second caught fire and spurted flame. We returned to the chicken coop happy.

On the morning of October 1, the Underground chief for the district came to see us. He told me that there was a British agent in the area who would like to see me, and that I was to leave immediately, but I would not be returning.

The night before I was asked if one of the sergeants could stay to instruct the Underground in the use of new weapons which were being dropped; and also to organize and lead the Underground in guerrilla raids against the enemy.

Sergeant Banwell said he would like to stay. I told Tex that it might be a long time before he would see Kettley and me again. He liked this type of warfare, he said, and wanted to remain behind. (Little did I know when I left Tex seventy miles from our nearest troops that he would twice try to escape and the second time be taken prisoner of war.)

I thanked my hosts, and with Olaf, the local chief, one other man, and Kettley, we began our bicycle trip. Where we were going, I did not know. I only knew that we were heading south.

We cycled along roads where Germans passed us freely and soon we stopped at another farmhouse. Here we picked up an aerial gunner who had crashed several days ago nearby. With our bicycle convoy now increased to five we proceeded on our way. An hour later we turned down a deserted road which twisted through a forest until it came to a large farm in a clearing. There were about twenty chicken coops in front of a big farm building. Olaf, the local chief, who took us here, led me to one of the chicken coops and knocked. A voice answered. Olaf spoke something and the door was unbolted from the inside and we entered.

It was the most amazing chicken coop I have ever been in. The walls were covered with white, thick, sound-absorbing panelling. There were two rooms, and in the far room I could see a huge downy bed covered with sheets, with a big comforter lying neatly folded on the top. The rooms were brightly lit and the blinds drawn. In the room I was in there was a wireless set and an operator working it. He paid no attention to us.

A tall man with horn-rimmed spectacles and a British uniform greeted me.

"You're Lieutenant Heaps, aren't you? I'm Captain King."

There was a faint trace of a French accent in his voice.

"Olaf told me you and the Sergeant have escaped. How long do you think it will be before the Airborne catch up with me?" He toyed with the rims of his glasses.

I explained that all the Airborne had been evacuated several nights ago. He seemed disappointed. It meant that he would be here many months instead of several weeks. He had dropped a week ago with two other men and thought he was sure to be overrun by the Airborne troops. (Eight months later I learned that Captain King had finally come through the enemy lines and reached our troops.)

I questioned him eagerly. I asked him if the Dutch could get me through the German lines and explained that it would probably be necessary to establish an escape line back to our own troops, as there were several hundred airborne troops still on this side of the river. Some arrangements must be made for getting them out, we thought.

He said he would arrange for a guide to take me out, and at the same time establish a route for the remainder. He would wire my name back to London so that our troops could be notified that I would be making the attempt. Kettley was to remain behind until the success or failure of the escape was made known.

That night the air gunner remained with Capt. King, and Kettley and I were taken to a Dutch farm in the neighbourhood, where we were fed by a kind farmer. The farmer was proud to have us and we were proud to be his guests. He treated us as his sons, and later offered to adopt me as he claimed I looked like a Dutchman. I refused at the time. At night we would sit about the fire and listen in on a radio, disguised as a cupboard, to the BBC. All the Dutchmen had a radio hidden away somewhere.

Next day Bep visited us. She was tall, blonde and pretty. Bep was a woman who had been a courier in the Underground for many years. It was her daily duty to bicycle through German troops and vehicle concentrations, make maps of German positions and carry daily, secret documents through the German lines. She could be shot almost any minute of any day if she were caught. But she never was.

On October 3, I returned to Capt. King. He had some important maps and documents for our troops. I put them in my stockings. One was a map elaborately done of German positions in this area; the other told in detail about German strength and the quality of the troops in Holland. I felt as if I were playing a role in a Hitchcock spy film.

Bep took me back to the farm where we had another fond goodbye with the farmer and his wife, collected Kettley and were on our way again. After two hours cycling over narrow Dutch paths and after crossing a road filled with German troops and transport, we reached a little crossroad on some high ground in the middle of a wood. Here we met a Dutchman called Pete. He spoke hardly any English, we no Dutch, but we got along fine. Pete had brought his girl friend along to see us. We shook hands, then we left the two young women. After we had cycled for a few moments Bep caught up to us.

"Here," she said. And she gave me a little Dutch-English dictionary. "This will help you." Then she gave me a black-and-white checkered scarf which I still have.

And she was off again with her girl friend. A very fine woman was Bep, and she has lived to see Holland liberated.

Pete stopped at a farmhouse where a hot meal was waiting for us. And then he went on to collect a revolver for me from an Underground storage point. While we were having lunch a very suave Dutchman entered the house and began to speak to me in perfect English.

"You boys crossing the line? Should have an excellent chance of getting through." Then he produced a map from his stocking and gave us the latest European war news, and showed me the exact German dispositions on the bank of the Rhine. When Pete returned I discovered that this man was an Agent, who had been operating in Holland for several years. Then Pete handed Kettley and me a revolver each, and we said goodbye to our hosts.

After another hour of cycling we could see the bank of the Rhine. We went through a gate on the edge of a field and began to walk our machines. We were careful, for all ground within a mile of the river was forbidden to civilians. When we reached the river we saw no one but two young men on the far bank gazing indifferently across at us. Then a man approached. Pete said that this man would row us across the river. Pete then shook hands with us and left. We did not even have time to thank him.

We crossed the river, without seeing a German, at three o'clock in the afternoon in a rowboat. It was much easier to row across the Rhine than to swim it, but this was only our first water barrier. Twenty-five miles to the south of the Rhine lay the river Waal. This was the river line defended strongly by the Germans.

When our boat touched down on the far bank, the two indifferent Dutchmen, whom we had seen lolling about on the shore, suddenly came to life. They made motions for us to follow them up the bank, and led us through an apple orchard to the back door of a house, which we entered. One of the young men was twenty. He was called Jop, and was small, with blond hair. Jop was the leader of the two. The other man was older and kept outside the house on lookout.

We were given tea by Jop's grandmother, and then she gave us a glass of advocaat. She was a very excitable woman, but very glad to have us in her house. She somehow felt she was doing something to defeat the Germans. She was cheating the Germans out of having Kettley and myself, and she liked doing that. Whenever I asked Jop if we could get through the lines, he would draw a slim finger across his throat and say, "It is like killing self dead." We were not encouraged.

When we finished tea I went out into the woodshed which was in front of the house. Only a few Germans passed by, but I noticed that most of them were Gestapo men. Suddenly one looked my way and saw me. Instinctively I moved back into the shadow of the shed. I had forgotten for the moment that I was in civilian clothes. He only glanced in at me and passed on. Then I went back into the house again.

A few moments later Jop's grandmother ran excitedly over to us. "Deutches, Deutches!" she shouted. She was terrified.

Her daughter led us out to an apple pile. Our military tunics, which we always wore hidden under our civilian clothes, we took off and hid under the apples. Then we left the house and hid in the orchard.

Presently the old lady came out. She was laughing. They were only after eggs, she was explaining, and were gone now. We were certain that they were not after eggs, as three days ago the Underground told us the Germans had been looking for us with police dogs. We decided to leave as soon as we could.

At suppertime that night we were joined by two of the most scholarly-looking gentlemen I have ever met. They were the two most unlikely people one would choose as members of the Underground. But Kettley and I had long since discovered that loyalty, principle and courage had no special relation to the shape of someone's nose or the contours of one's face.

The small man, who said grace before cracking the eggshell, was the very soul of humility. The other man was in his early twenties, was unassuming, and appeared to be a typical Dutch undergraduate. The man with the glasses was one of the leaders of the Betuwe area, which is the name of the district between the Rhine and the Waal rivers in Holland.

He told us that the German line now ran between the narrowest part of those two rivers, in a direction twenty miles east of Maurik (where we were now). It was opposed by a similar British line also between the two rivers and running north and south. It was almost an impossibility for two non-Dutch-speaking people to get through here. The only way to reach our lines was to cross the Waal near Tiel. Here the Germans had not been particularly vigilant during the past few weeks.

That night we were to move to a house nearer to Tiel, from where I would attempt to cross the Waal with a Dutch guide. Kettley would be left behind to follow if our crossing was successful. He in turn would be followed by stray paratroopers and airmen who had been caught behind the German lines, and especially by those who had been in the Arnhem operation.

Before dusk five of us left by bicycle for the next stage of the journey. We travelled by a circuitous route to avoid suspicion. And, although our destination was only five miles away, it took us almost two hours to cycle there. It was timed so that we could arrive at the house just at dark. Ahead of us about twenty yards always cycled our lookout man.

The house we came to was almost halfway between the river Rhine and the Waal, and was itself situated on a trickling stream known as the Linge. It was a large rambling house with a big orchard behind it, and lay on the edge of a very small village.

A man who looked like a typical country squire came out and greeted us. He was the resistance chief for the whole area between the two rivers. I never discovered what his real name was during the three days I was with him. The name he used with us was Ebbins.

After we put our bicycles away we entered the house. It was beautifully furnished. Mr. Ebbins lived here with his wife and his grandmother under normal conditions, but now he had many guests.

Inside the house I met an American Air Force pilot who had been shot down on the first day of the supply drop, and with him was a British paratrooper who suffered from a fractured leg. Upstairs I discovered a Jewish family who had been living here for a year in fear and secrecy.

During the day his house was used as the meeting place for the Resistance. In the basement he had large stores of arms and ammunition. In fact, it was used for too many purposes, and was certain to be discovered. Kettley and I were certain it was only a matter of time. (Two months later his house was burned to the ground by the Germans and his family cast into a concentration camp.)

The people here were growing a little careless, for they believed liberation was only days away. Each day there I was asked, "When is the Tommy coming?" It was not until ten months later that our troops came here to stay.

Next afternoon I met another young, blond Dutchman in the Underground called Pete. He spoke good English. We discussed the possibility of getting across the river at Tiel. He said he would go that afternoon and see what the prospects were like, and that he would be back to see me tomorrow morning.

I told the Resistance chief that I had some important documents which must get across the river to our troops as soon as possible. That afternoon I met a young man in the Underground named Frans DeVilder, with whom I later became great friends. He would swim the Waal tonight with the documents, and a note which was addressed to the nearest Allied Headquarters. In the note, among other things, I mentioned that I would be crossing the river some time this week either by swimming or by rowboat, and to be on the watch. That night Frans DeVilder swam the Waal with the secret papers and passed them to the nearest Allied

Headquarters, which happened to be the Guards Armoured Division stationed near Nijmegen.

The next day, October 4, Pete returned from his reconnaissance of the river. He said two of us could go with him. The aerial gunner, who had worked with Capt. King, was now with me, and I decided that Kettley would stay to direct things here, and the Gunner would accompany me over the river tonight.

That night I thanked my host for everything he had done, checked my revolver, and set out with the Gunner and Pete on bicycles for Tiel. Before we got to Tiel my machine had a flat tyre and I was forced to walk with it. As I walked it through Tiel I passed a group of Germans who were taking photographs of each other on the street. I had to stop to go through them, as they were crowding the road and blocking it. As I began to walk through one German soldier spoke to me, demanding something. I jumped on my bicycle and pedalled as fast as I could down the street. I did not dare look behind until I caught up with Pete and the Gunner who were far ahead. When we had gone almost a mile I looked behind. No one was following.

At last we passed through the city and reached the country around the river area and began to walk with our bicycles along the side of a canal. Ahead about two hundred yards was the summer dike, and on the other side was the river Waal. Across the river lay our freedom.

Pete stopped fifty yards ahead and told us to remain where we were. He went down the side of the dike road we were on into a little house on the left. Soon he came back and beckoned us to join him.

When we arrived at the house we met the bargeman who was to help us. He was extremely nervous and was inclined to let his teeth chatter when he spoke. If he was caught, it meant his life.

About a hundred yards ahead was a lock on the canal which we had to pass over in order to get to the dike road, which ran parallel to the river. On the other side of the lock was a house. There was a German machine-gun post and two or three Germans who were on guard at the house. At present only one German was on guard at the house, and two were manning the machine-gun post on a piece of open ground near the river. Every now and then they would put a burst across the water. The road we were on ran along the left side of the canal leading down to the river.

We had to time the crossing of the lock, from left to right, exactly. Pete watched.

"Okay, now," he said.

Pete, myself, the Gunner and the bargeman began to saunter, with a forced effort at nonchalance, down to the lock. I took an apple out of my pocket and began to eat it without appetite.

We crossed the lock as the guard was talking to a Dutch woman, whom he spoke to at this time every night. The guard turned to me for some unknown reason and spoke. My mouth was full of apple.

"Glub, glub, glub," I answered.

The guard was content. Then Pete pointed to the side of the dike. I moved there quickly. Evidently the guard had told me to watch out for machine-gun fire, as the damned British were shooting at everything they saw on the top of the dike.

We walked about three hundred yards alongside of the dike and stopped. The bargeman and Pete, I noticed, both had very pasty white complexions. Why I did not shiver with fright, I do not honestly know.

Pete timed it again, and we scrambled over the top of the dike, to creep up behind a little hill which led toward the part of the river where the barge was moored. We boarded the barge and hid in the cabin. We were now to wait until complete darkness before we could take the rowboat tied to the side of the barge across the river. The bargeman had permission to return to his barge that night, and we would see him again before we crossed.

About half an hour after dark we were joined by the bargeman again. He had a crippled little man with him who had paid a very large sum of money to leave German territory. He was to come with us tonight.

Pete told us to move quickly as the Germans were on their way down to the barge. We jumped over the side and into the boat, and Pete took the oars and began to row out into the middle of the stream. The crippled man kept telling me that I must save him if the boat sank. He kept on repeating this.

The Germans put a burst of machine-gun fire on the river. They were firing blindly at us. It was too dark for them to see us. Just as our rowboat arrived at the far shore, the Germans shot a mortar flare up into the night above the river. Everything for a moment was as brilliant as day, but we were across. They were too late.

Twice within six days I had been exhilarated in a way which was incomparable to anything I have ever experienced before. Once was when I dropped off the train on the way to Frankfort and realized that I was free; and lay for one brief moment unbelieving as the train passed away forever out of my life. And now it was here upon our own shore. I had come through the lines in eighteen exciting days. Today was the most beautiful October 5th in my life.

There were no troops in this area as it was No-Man's-Land. We deposited the crippled man at a Dutch house. The people told us our troops were just along the dike road on the way to Nijmegen. On the dike road we met Frans DeVilder with some of his Underground friends. They had a civilian car waiting for us. Everybody was excited. Frans had delivered the secret maps, documents, and my message yesterday evening, and our own troops should be aware of our arrival.

Some of our troops evidently advanced this far in the daytime with the armoured cars, but at night everything withdrew back into Nijmegen.

After half an hour's driving our big Buick stopped at a house. I went inside and met the local Resistance chief. His name was Dr. Van Hooker. He was a kindly old doctor who was the Resistance leader in this area. He fed us and gave us clean beds to sleep in. Everybody was deliriously happy, especially me.

Next morning I was taken to the Guards Armoured Division at Nijmegen, then to Corps and Army.

After a process of Intelligence interrogation which I had to be subjected to, I was finally removed to Eindhoven, where I met the friends I was to work with during the next ten months, in the extrication of several hundred paratroops still hiding in the Arnhem area. At Eindhoven I met Major Neave and Major Fraser and a lady reporter named Mrs. Hemingway (Martha Gellhorn), who was the wife of the novelist, Ernest Hemingway. And that night the Gunner and myself were given a banquet.

Next day I was removed to Brussels from where I was flown back to England.

The papers of England in the traditional manner of paying homage to a devastating, but heroic defeat, had been very liberal in the publicity which was given to the Arnhem episode. The air was still humming with it.

While in England I met General Urquhart at the War Office, and told him as best I could what had happened to the remainder of the force. I told him I had been asked to return to Holland in a few days. He gave me his full consent to carry on with the job I had already begun. And much to my surprise told me I was the only one to return after the remnants had been evacuated on that unfortunate night by the Canadian Engineers.

The rest of the day I spent re-equipping myself generously from the stores of the Special Air Service in London.

That day I saw the strength return for the Division, after the evacuation. Out of eight hundred other ranks and forty officers, ten other ranks and two officers besides myself had returned from my parachute battalion. The lists read like this for the other battalions as well.

That night I spent writing letters, sending cablegrams to Canada, and thinking.

Events were too freshly impressed upon my mind as yet to appraise them in their proper perspective. I only knew that I had been fortunate and thousands of others had been terribly unfortunate. I felt a surge of confidence come over me and knew that at twenty-two I had found myself. In eighteen days I had come home again from my wanderings in Holland. I felt unbelievably lucky.

II

SOMEWHERE, WANDERING BEHIND THE GERMAN LINES, in Holland, were two brigadiers, six colonels, about sixty other officers, and at least five hundred non-commissioned ranks.

Our big difficulty in bringing these people back would be the crossing of the Rhine River which separated our troops from the Germans.

At this time the Allied Armies had liberated roughly the southern half of Holland. They held the river line along the Maas in western Holland. And where the river Maas approached the Waal farther west there was No-Man's-Land. This is where I had crossed the Waal near Tiel. From here east our reconnaissance units held the river line of the Waal.

Running north about twenty miles, and roughly parallel to the Waal, was the River Rhine or Lek. Still farther east our troops had a line between the Waal and the Rhine which opposed a similar German line to the west. Therefore there was a space between the Rhine and Waal occupied by our troops. The main axis of this territory between the rivers ran from Nijmegen, north to a little place called Elst, which almost sat on the Rhine itself. Across the river from Elst was Arnhem.

When I arrived back in Holland from England I met Major Neave who was in charge of the clandestine operations. I was to work between the area roughly from Tiel to Nijmegen with my Dutch Underground friends.

Also in the interim while I had been back to England, I learned Kettley had come through the lines at Tiel. Evidently he had passed through two days previously.

During the next several weeks I worked with my Dutch friends Pete, Frans, and Dr. Van Hooker, establishing a ferry service across the Waal on dark, moonless nights. During one week Frans swam the Waal five times bringing across valuable documents and information about our survivors. We had our little defeats and our little victories.

One night the door of my little house opened in No-Man's-Land and there was Frans. He had just rowed across the river that night from Tiel with a paratroop officer. It turned out to be Lt.-Col. Dobie, my own commander. We were very glad to see each other again. Colonel Dobie had a plan by which he hoped to rescue from the far bank of the Rhine two hundred airborne evaders.[2] He asked me to help him.

Next night I accompanied Lt.-Colonel Dobie to a secret telephone terminus near Nijmegen. Here from a modern, well-furnished room he spoke to a British paratroop major who was in hiding twenty miles behind the enemy lines and beyond the river Rhine. With him the final plans for the mass escape were completed. Next day Lt.-Colonel Dobie asked me to move to the Headquarters of the 101st American Airborne Division. They were to supply the men and the fire plan for this clandestine operation. The next day the General commanding the British Corps, which had the Americans attached, came to put his imprimatur upon the final plans. Everything was in readiness for the following evening. That day I moved in with the American Parachute Battalion who were to do the job.

---

[2] People who are not behind the enemy lines on official business are divided into two categories: evaders — men who have been left behind the lines after a withdrawal as was the case in Arnhem; escapers — men who have been taken prisoner and escaped from the enemy. To avoid confusion everybody caught behind the lines is referred to as an evader.

The American 101st Airborne Division had come up to the river Rhine after the British troops withdrew with the survivors of the First Airborne Division.

Across the river from the Americans lay the familiar bank where I had been just over a month ago. A little to the east again lay Oosterbeek and Arnhem. We were to cross the river several miles west of Oosterbeek.

At midnight the following night small bands of paratroops coming down from the north would link up with other small parties at Dutch Underground posts, and the forward element of the big party would give three white dashes when they reached the north bank of the river. Starting at fifteen minutes to midnight a Bofors gun would fire fifteen tracer shells in a straight line across the river. This was the axis of advance for the paratroops coming to the bank of the Rhine. This was to be repeated at half-hour intervals.

When we in turn saw the light flash on the far bank, we were to cross the river with forty assault boats and gather up the two hundred evaders and dash back as quickly as we could. A small party of American paratroops were to cross on the flanks and cover the sides with machine-gun fire in case we were interfered with. The British would supply the assault boats. The artillery were, in the advent of trouble, to seal off the back of our little square with a very heavy artillery and mortar barrage. The known enemy strength was thought to be several companies, which were scattered in unknown positions on the far bank, back, however, from the river. The Americans were responsible for the organization and administration of the evaders when they returned to our lines. The Dutch Resistance would guide the evaders down little-known paths to the edge of the Rhine.

At ten o'clock on the night of the operation everything was in readiness. The assault boats were in place in some trees, a hundred feet from the river edge. My job was to ensure that they were launched as quickly as possible, and, when I reached the far bank, to contact the evaders and direct them back to the boats.

It was very quiet out and very dark. There was no moon in the sky and the atmosphere vibrated with a tension and expectancy. Everyone waited, quietly, excitedly. A pig in a barn near the river squealed several times. A few miles back from the river we could see the flaming paths of the "Moaning Minnies" as they screeched up into the sky. We could hear them land a mile behind us. Then the staccato cracking of the Bofors gun was heard. Tracers streaked across the sky on the axis of advance. The tracers spun a thread of brilliant light across the black heaven above the river. It was now fifteen minutes to midnight.

I looked at my watch. Now the hands were perched on midnight. I looked up again across the river, and far to the east I saw the winking of a light. I raced down to the river. I jumped into the boat farthest east along the river bank and shouted to the remainder to follow. Colonel Dobie was already out in the stream. The river was crossed in a minute.

On the far side the bank was quiet and foreboding. Other assault boats were coming up alongside of me. I took two Americans with me and we headed carefully east along the bank toward the light we had seen. It came on again, and it winked feebly at us. Suddenly from a bush on my left a white Verey light illumined the sky. I could see our troops flattened out on the bank to the left of me. Everybody was waiting like myself until the darkness enveloped us again. We waited in the dark for a minute and nothing else happened. We got up and walked another two hundred yards along the grassy land above the bank in the direction the light signal had come from. We heard noise in the distance. It was the muffled sound of feet crunching on wet grass. We laid down flat upon the ground and waited. Then into sight on the very edge of the river came a very long line of men marching in single file. Some had civilian clothes on, others wore the torn remains of a battledress. I overtook them and came to the front of the column. There was a major at the head, and behind him was a paratroop brigadier. I pointed to where the boats were waiting. Then I left them and returned to pick up the stragglers who were wounded or too weak to have kept up with the column.

Half an hour later the last of the evaders were on their way across the river. Before I left I turned my head for a last glimpse of the shoreline and I knew how frightened the Germans must be. They had not let out one sound or fired one bullet at us during the entire time we had been on their shore. I looked at my watch. It was now fifteen minutes past one in the morning. We had been walking around in front of the Germans for seventy minutes and no one had bothered us. It was almost unbelievable.

My mind turned back to the last time I had been washed up on this beach, tired and exhausted. This time it had been different. The Rhine was becoming an old friend.

The Americans could hardly have had the reception of the evaders better organized. When the evaders disembarked on the far shore they followed a white tape laid upon the ground. This took them to a house where they had a hot meal and a cup of rum. Another white tape led them to the medical room where those who needed attention were quickly looked after. Another white tape took them to transport which was waiting for them on the road. Within half an hour of landing one hundred and forty tired people, who had been behind the lines for two months, were sleeping soundly in a hospital in Nijmegen.

That night I rode back in my jeep to see an American lieutenant who had crossed the river with Colonel Dobie. I had had a very pleasant two days with my American friends, and tonight the climax of all our preparations had been reached and achieved. I said goodbye to my friends and left for Nijmegen. I was happy and went to bed when I reached my billet.

Next morning I visited the hospital. I had taken with me Frans, whom Colonel Dobie was to take back to England that afternoon by plane. Frans was to realize his great dream and become a pilot in the Dutch Air Force.

Since I was free and unattached, I said goodbye to Major Fraser, under whom I had been working with Major Neave, and decided to return that afternoon by plane to England.

From some of the survivors I learned that Tex Banwell had not made any attempt to come through the lines, but was still working with the Dutch Resistance where I had left him. This was distressing news. I also found out the whereabouts of many of my friends, for there were still over a hundred of the Airborne behind the lines hidden by the Dutch Resistance. The longer these people were behind the lines, the greater became their chance of capture and the less their chance of escape.

That afternoon I took off for England, and that night I slept at the airport where my plane landed. Next morning I learned that the evaders were to fly to England that day, and hoped to see them come in. But their course was changed at the last moment, and they landed somewhere north in Lincolnshire. From here they would all be specially despatched to their homes.

Later on that week I saw General Urquhart again, and told him what had happened during the past month when I was away. Since Major Neave's organization had asked me to return, the General gave me carte blanche. This was the type of Army life I enjoyed — roaming almost at will, yet with a purpose, over the continent.

Since Sergeant Kettley was in England I put in a request through the Airborne Headquarters that he follow me out to Holland. The request was granted. I then acquired a jeep and took it with me to an American aerodrome near London, where I convinced the Transport Officer I had urgent duty to complete in Europe. The jeep and myself both boarded a Dakota and took off that afternoon for Brussels.

Two hours later I was in Brussels, driving through its downtown section. The streets, the streetcars and crowds reminded me of New York's downtown section. The crowds were gay in the cafés and were still celebrating their newfound freedom. Christmas was only a few weeks away and there was a joyous mood in the people. Since I was in no great hurry I decided to stop at the Atlanta Hotel where the officers' club was located.

While I was downstairs checking my hat an officer approached me from the foyer. It was Hal Foster. It was marvellous meeting him again. Hal, I noticed, was now a captain. As we proceeded toward the dining room I inquired about his life in the Dorsets. When we were seated he spoke. "I stayed with the Dorsets until I was practically the only original officer left in the battalion. We got a brand-new company commander from England after the old one was killed. He was a great guy. And he had to get it the first night he was in action." He leaned back wearily in his chair.

"I notice you're with the Desert Rats now," I said.

"Yes, I joined the Seventh Armoured Division when I got out of the hospital. Got wounded, you know." Then he remarked, "The big push, it seems, is just around the corner. When it starts our motor battalion will be right at the front of it." His face was set in tight lines when he finished talking.

We spent most of the evening discussing what had happened since we had last met and remembering almost forgotten acquaintances. Hal, to me, represented the best type of Infantryman: the man in this war who knows no rest; the man who must meet the enemy eye to eye and root him out of his slit-trench. There are not many real Infantrymen who go home again. I left Hal with a promise to look him up again at the first opportunity I had.

Later on that evening I located Major Neave who took me to one of the exclusive hotels where he kept a flat. Here he discussed the future plans. It was early next morning when he was through and I went to bed ready to leave that same day for Nijmegen. The trip to Nijmegen took six hours and I moved into one of the luxurious houses which the Organization had requisitioned.

Major Neave had for some time played with the idea of evacuating a number of paratroops and airmen from behind the enemy lines, in much the same manner as Colonel Dobie and I had carried out the evacuation several weeks ago. The American 101st Airborne Division was still holding the river bank and knew the preparations necessary for such a job.

Major Neave was in constant touch with "Dick", who was our contact man operating behind the German lines. With Dick another rescue was planned and code-named "Pegasus". Since the secret telephone terminus behind the German lines had been discovered, communications now were not as direct as they had been. After several weeks of planning, replanning and revising, however, a conference was held at the headquarters of the 101st Airborne Division. The only major difference between this plan and the other would be that this time the Canadian Engineers who rescued the survivors from Arnhem would do the crossing of the river in their storm boats. (Storm boats are flat-bottomed boats about twenty-five feet long, powered by a large outboard motor.)

Major Tucker who was in charge of the storm boats would cross first when the red light signal was flashed from the far bank. The evaders would number about one hundred and fifty men who had been collected by the Dutch Underground from all parts of occupied Holland during the past month. There would be a concentration point in a wood six miles from the river where they would form up in single file after being briefed, and then proceed down to the river with several Dutch guides at the front of the column.

The night of the operation we gathered in the cellar of a house used as a command post, which was situated a little way back from the river behind a dike. It was a cold, raw night and Major Fraser looked like a Greek warrior as he paced nervously up and down the small cellar with his American helmet set down well over his ears. Major Neave in his careless Oxford accent would remark occasionally that something should happen soon and give an awkward little laugh, then would go back to sleep in the corner again. At midnight we were all outside to witness the twelve cracks of the Bofors gun and watch the tracers spin their line of advance to the far shore. All that night we waited and there was no light to be seen from the other side. It was almost morning as I went wearily home to snatch a few hours' sleep before returning to the command post that same evening for a further vigil.

When I arrived next day at the river, I was told that a man with a thick Irish accent had been shouting across the river to the Americans to come and get him. He shouted that he was there with two Dutchmen and there were no Germans about. He appeared several times before dark, yelling and gesticulating to us, and just before night fell this warrior with the Irish accent disappeared into a clump of bushes by the river's edge.

When it was dark Major Tucker launched a storm boat and crossed the river. Over the "Walky-Talky" he garbled something to me about capturing Germans and Dutchmen, and the conversation was mangled by odd shouts and weird cursing in a foreign language which I took to be Irish. Ten minutes later the storm boat came back. Major Tucker arrived back with two nondescript characters in civilian clothes, who had their hands above their heads. In the cellar the Irishman was trying to explain that his name was O'Casey, and that he and the Dutchman had been a part of Operation Pegasus. When O'Casey went to refer to the Dutchman for evidence he was nowhere to be seen, and was finally found reviving himself by taking liberal swigs from a jug of rum, after which be passed out cold. Before the Irishman became drunk by a similar act of revival, we discovered that the column had been discovered by a lone German sentry as it wended its way toward the river. The sentry had given the alarm. There was a panic. The column dispersed into a wood close by, which was mortared and machine-gunned and finally searched by the Germans. Most of the men who sought safety in the woods were finally captured or killed. Some few had forged their way on to the river and O'Casey and the Dutch guide were of this class.

A few hours later on that night a light winked weakly on and off from across the river about half a mile downstream. One of the observation posts phoned in that there was some shouts and sound of rifle shots from where the light had shone. Any light which came from the far bank might be some of our own troops which had slipped through the German cordon.

An American lieutenant approached his American colonel in the cellar, and anxiously said, "Sir, there is only one sure way to get those men back on the far shore and that's by canoe. Let me go and I'll bring those British boys back."

"The current is pretty swift, Dixon. What makes you think you can do it?"

The lieutenant said squarely, "I can handle anything with a paddle that floats. I'm from Florida and I was brought up with a canoe on the bayous."

"Okay, Dixon," said the Colonel a little wearily. "Have a try at it."

I was in contact with Dixon on the "Walky-Talky" when he landed on the other side of the river. He whispered back that he had located a British paratrooper and an airman. After that the set went dead. The last thing I ever heard about the young man from Florida was when a post several miles downstream reported hearing cries of help from the river and saw a shape which resembled a canoe being borne swiftly out of control past the western extremity of our positions. All that night at irregular intervals there were lights and cries from the far bank, but we knew that many of these lights and shouts were ruses used by the Germans in hope that we would cross over. In the early morning hours the Germans began to fire their machine-guns above the dike, and finally, when dawn completely opened up into morning, the river and the Germans were still.

The American Colonel came out of the cellar humming softly to himself, and gazed through the early morning fuzz across to the far bank and grew silent. Then he turned to me and shook his head.

Major Fraser appeared from the cellar tired and uncertain, and gazed into the fuzz across the river and saw nothing move on the other shore.

On the road behind me Major Tucker and his Engineers carried the heavy storm boats back to the concentration area. Then the Germans began to mortar us, and everyone trudged wearily home.

Pegasus had not paid off.

After several days of inactivity in Nijmegen I moved off west to a big white house which was set a quarter of a mile back from the river Waal. Across the river from the house was the town of Tiel from which I had escaped several months ago. The area the house was in was almost a No-Man's-Land patrolled occasionally by elements of British and Canadian Reconnaissance Units. Once or twice during each week a German patrol would cross to our side of the river in an effort to seize a prisoner, or to ambush a lone reconnaissance car travelling on one of the wooded roads at night. Sometimes the German patrol would take back a prisoner and sometimes the German patrol would fail to return to their own lines.

Our large white stucco house originally belonged to a Dutch collaborator who had been released from jail because of insufficient evidence. The collaborator was a long, thin-nosed man who was meek and servile now. We put him and his family in the rear portion of the house and occupied the rest ourselves. In spite of being close to the enemy we enjoyed the luxuries of home. We had central heating, electric lights and hot baths. The meals were really enormous, because in addition to our own rations we liberally helped ourselves to the almost inexhaustible larder of chickens, geese, rabbits and jarred fruit which we discovered in the cellar. It was always a strange contrast to leave this beautiful home to be launched by boat on the dark river against the enemy.

Several days later I was joined by Kettley who had been sent out from England.

The white house was located near the village of Dreumel, where one of the squadrons of the Seventh Canadian Reconnaissance Regiment had its headquarters. Here began a long friendship with Major Davolpie, the Squadron Commander, and his second-in-command, Captain Doug Johnston.

On cold winter nights in December and January we would sit around the warm hearth in my house and relate to each other our adventures, and talk about home. On other evenings I would make reconnaissance trips along the river bank with Kettley to find launching places for our boats. On one such night as this I was accompanied to the river by Doug Johnston, who had with him a French lad called Louis, whom Doug had acquired on his romp with his Reconnaissance cars across France. It seemed that Louis was very adept with a wire noose he carried, with which he deftly and quickly strangled, collected and carted away a young cow who had foolishly wandered. Doug would patrol the river bank in his great sheepskin coat while Louis would search the ground around for cows. Louis was not as particular as his captain for he would often waylay young chickens as well.

Working in close association with me on the river was Captain Peter Vickery, whose job it was to organize the Dutch Underground and build it into a unified fighting force. Peter was a man of character and sincerity and for relaxation he collected weapons and Germans. He was a tall, languorous Englishman who had a thin scraggly moustache.

On moonless nights Peter would cross the Waal to meet friends of his in the Underground behind the German lines. Then sometimes during the next day I would hear an explosion in the early hours of the morning and knew that Peter Vickery had been at work. Some days later Peter would suddenly reappear in my life and quietly tell how he had blown another bridge or a section of a railway track. Sometimes he would tell of a scuffle with the Germans and show me a new Luger or automatic weapon. Peter never made any show of bravery, but was always quiet and dispassionate about what he had done. (Several months later I learned with sorrow how Peter had been killed in an aeroplane crash in Italy, on his way out to Burma.)

It was through Peter that I met one of the unforgettable characters of the Dutch Intelligence Service. This was Lieutenant Andre Koch. Andre Koch was likely to appear at any place at any time of day or night, and to expect him to appear when he was in need could be considered as pure folly. At this time any enterprising Dutchman who had escaped from occupied Holland to England and hobnobbed with the London Dutch Government always returned to Holland considerably enriched by a vague prestige; and they carried with them a glamour which was denied to their colleagues who had been working for strenuous years in the Underground of Holland.

Koch was distinguished by having escaped from Holland through Belgium, France, Spain and finally Gibraltar where he was picked up by a Dutch submarine and taken to England. Since this time Koch always carried in the pocket of his much over-sized greatcoat a very long-barrelled, silent pistol which fired a bullet no larger than the head of a nail.

Koch, Peter Vickery and myself would several times during the course of a week wait on the stone promontory across the way from Tiel for our Underground couriers to bring us news from the occupied territory. Sometimes it would be Jan van Elzen who would come across, and sometimes the river would cast up for us an inquisitive German in a canoe who was eager to spy on our troops. We never knew who would come across the river.

After we left the river for the night we would gather at my house where Koch would discourse upon the glory and future of Holland; his long, thin body stooped over as he threw his arms about in wild, gesticulating motions, after which he would puff furiously at his cigarette which perpetually dangled from the side of his mouth. While this went on the Germans would usually be mortaring our house from across the river, as Koch would invariably forget to put the blackouts up in his room.

It was late in the month of December that I met again Jan van Elzen, a courageous-hearted Dutchman who had played a very prominent role in the Dutch Resistance.

I first met Jan behind the enemy lines when I stayed at Mr. Ebbins' house on the outskirts of Tiel, where Jan was engaged in smuggling weapons into German territory for use by the Underground. Four times every week Jan would canoe across the Waal with his cargo, and with his friend Grisel, would carry the arms by night to a secret storage house in Tiel.

It was customary for Jan to disappear for several weeks and suddenly reappear at my house on the Waal with a request for food, medicine and arms to take back across the river with him the following night.

One night Jan, Grisel and two unknown Dutchmen decided to embark on an adventure which would be of considerable value to the Army from the viewpoint of Intelligence. They were to row across the river, and at the same time lay a cable which would have a secret terminus from a lonely brick factory on our shore to a brick factory on the enemy bank. The brick factory on our side was in a No-Man's-Land which was seldom visited by the Germans, and it was from here that Jan and his party would start.

A little before midnight the moon sank behind thick clouds, to disappear for the night, and our three jeeps climbed to the dike road from my house and went down the snowy path towards the brick factory. At the factory we met our two Dutch sentries who reported that no enemy patrols had been in the vicinity that evening. The water was swirling on the river and you could hear the swift charge of the current meeting a stone promontory downstream.

The two Signallers were setting up drums of wire cable on the river edge which would unwind as the rowboat pulled out from this shore toward the far bank. Jan van Elzen would be on the telephone in the rowboat and the Signal officer would be on our end of the phone in contact with Jan as the cable unwound. The skipper, a hardy, weather-tanned bargeman, would row the boat to the brick factory on the far shore, the exact position of which he knew well in any weather, night or day. When the far bank was reached Jan would test the phone once again and then hide it in a brick kiln, cover the wire over with dirt and reappear on schedule at midnight, two nights later.

The Signal officer whispered "Hello, Jan," and Jan whispered back from the boat. Then Jan cast off into the river. For half an hour we had contact with Jan, then the wire snagged on the river bed and personal contact with Jan was gone until I saw him again in the following spring.

While Jan was in Tiel, supplying us by courier with information about German troop movements, his house was raided by the S.D. (a Dutch Quisling Police modelled on the Gestapo) and his wife and two children taken as hostages. Jan, fortunately, was not home at the time of the raid. In Jan's house a British pilot was discovered in hiding and the death penalty was imposed upon Jan's family.

Jan rallied to his side ten trusted friends and planned to rescue his wife from the jail in Tiel. One early dawn Jan's small band struck, killing the guards and releasing his wife and two children. That same night Jan and his family started their hundred-mile trek by cart and foot westward across Holland to Sliedrecht. Then from Sliedrecht he rowed his family down the eight miles of Merwede River to the safety of our own lines, quietly bringing them to freedom.

But this was not enough for Jan, for in a few weeks the spirit of restlessness grew in him and he vanished again behind the lines to carry on his Underground activities of sabotage and espionage against the Germans.

In the early days of October, Major Fraser, accompanied by our communications expert, Morris Macmillan, came to see me at the big white house on the Waal. Morris used to visit me regularly in an effort to get behind the German lines. He disliked his job on communications and desired more excitement. Since the object of Major Fraser's visit this afternoon was to have me put two Dutch Agents across the river into enemy territory, Morris had come along in an effort to persuade Major Fraser to let him go. As usual, Morris was forbidden.

A few days later Morris and I were supplied with two Dutchmen by the Underground who would undertake the mission. One of these men was called Pete and the other one was named Leo. Both were in their early twenties.

Pete was blond and of medium height. He had been a student when war broke out and had been taken as a forced labourer to Germany. Once he escaped and returned, a hunted man, to Holland. A second time he was taken prisoner and shipped to Germany and again he escaped. Then he went underground and joined the Resistance movement. His family were across the river in German-occupied Tiel. He was determined and strong-willed like most of his comrades, and hated the Germans.

Leo was tall and very thin, and wore a thick-lensed pair of spectacles. He did not have too many original ideas and relied on Pete for leadership. And like Pete he was of a single purpose, which was to free Holland from the Germans.

After a ten-day course by Morris in the use of our special wireless set, Pete and Leo were ready for their infiltration. We waited four days for the moon period to change and then we were ready.

Along each river in Holland running parallel to one another there are two dikes. The dikes are about two hundred yards apart, and the one nearest the river proper is known as the summer dike and the one farther back is called the winter dike. In winter the river overflows the summer dike and reaches the winter dike. The water between the two dikes in winter time tends to recede and sometimes freeze, while the water in the main river flows on undisturbed. Such was the condition of the river when Leo and Pete made their first attempt.

My plan was to escort Leo and Pete to the summer dike with my motor-powered canoe, and from there cast them off.

On the night of the operation the air was fouled by a thick mist, and visibility was limited to a bare minimum.

The water between the two dikes had a trace of ice upon it. When the canoes reached the summer dike that night everything was coated with a thin layer of ice. Leo and Pete followed me with a paddle canoe.

Water had also frozen on our hands, which were numbed and almost useless. The two Dutchmen dragged their canoe onto the edge of the summer dike which protruded above the water, and then they shoved off into the misty night for Tiel, which was only two hundred yards away. Presently all you could hear was the soft swoosh of paddles carefully dipped into almost frozen water. And then there was only the river and the mist left.

In the motor canoe there was Newton, a Canadian Engineer, Kettley and myself. When Leo and Pete disappeared into the mist we turned about and started on our way back to the winter dike. The water was now covered with a layer of ice and we had to force a path back. Newton, thinking we were almost at the winter dike, put in the pontoons of the canoe. Then Kettley leaned a little too far to one side and our canoe overturned and we crashed through the ice into the water. We waded chest-deep in water, frozen and miserable, breaking ice as we went ahead and dragging our overturned canoe behind us. Once in a while we would disappear from sight into a deep spot beneath the water and reappear a moment later through the ice.

When we reached the winter dike and emerged from the water we quickly boarded our jeep and raced for home. We could not talk to one another because the water had strangled our speech. When we returned home we changed, took a hot bath and went directly to bed.

About four o'clock that morning there was a great banging on the front door. I arose, slung a tommy-gun over my shoulder and cautiously went to the door. Here were Leo and Pete. They both were almost frozen, their civilian clothes were rigid with ice, and their teeth chattered. They managed to tell me that when they reached the far bank they could hear Germans talking at the spot they were to land, and due to the mist on the river and the uncertainty of their position had decided to return. Leo had a bullet graze on his left thigh — one of our own troops fired at him before he had time to shout the password. They both were weary and bone-tired and went to bed. We would have to try again in a few days.

During the next week we collected more accurate data from our Agents regarding German positions on the far bank. Leo and Pete took a trip in an Auster observation plane high above the river and marked on their maps and in their minds the flooded area about Tiel. In this way they would know what ground to avoid after they landed.

The water about the river's edge was now beginning to freeze, and it would not be long until operations along the river would have to be abandoned for the winter. The night before we were to undertake the crossing, an unknown Dutchman swam the freezing waters from Tiel to our lines and from him we received much important information about German positions.

On the night of the operation, the air was cleared of mist and the moon would not appear until four o'clock in the morning. The temperature was below freezing and Leo and Pete were both anxious to set off.

The plan tonight would be slightly altered from the previous attempt. The power canoe would go out to the summer dike, trailed by the paddle canoe containing Leo and Pete, which in turn was followed by a rubber dinghy containing Lieutenant Cronyn, our Canadian Engineer officer and his Engineer sergeant. When we reached the summer dike my power canoe and the paddle canoe would be lifted over the dike, while the Engineer officer waited here for my power canoe to return after escorting Leo and Pete to Tiel.

Due to the swift river current in the Waal the power canoe must tow the paddle canoe to within a few feet of the far shore before casting it off. In the power canoe there would be Newton who operated the silent motor, Kettley who sat in the cockpit in the rear, holding the tow rope, and myself steering in the front cockpit. The course we were to take was a half a mile due west along the river edge, then due north. This would take us to an isolated area a little to the east of Tiel. I was to find my way back by means of a light operated by Lieutenant Cronyn, which I could see when I came within fifty feet of the summer dike.

We launched at midnight and our trip to the summer dike was uneventful. Leo and Pete were very cold in their civilian clothes. My hands were so numb that I could not feel the steering lines. At the summer dike we launched again into the main river and towed the paddle canoe swiftly downstream. It was a very dark night. Behind I could make out the Sapper trying to thaw his hands out by putting them near the motor. Kettley was covered by a thin sheet of ice from the spray and looked a little ill. In the paddle canoe, Pete had the haversack containing the set on his back and managed a faint smile. Leo was biting deep into his lower lip and was visibly frightened. Both knew the fate which would be theirs if they were caught and the suffering which would befall their families in occupied territory. Their risks were much greater than ours could ever be.

I pulled on the right steering line. Then I jerked it. It was stuck. I jerked it again and some of the ice broke loose, and the canoe slowly swung right toward the enemy bank. The Engineer cut the speed of the motor in half and we barely moved against the current. The dark shapeless mass which meant land ahead in the darkness was just in front now. We edged by degrees, carefully, very carefully to the shore and then swung broadside. Kettley cast Leo and Pete off and their canoe slipped away with the current in the darkness toward the bank. Suddenly our canoe jarred and the motor stopped. We were aground. Without a moment's hesitation Kettley stepped into the water up to his waist and pushed us off. The Sapper started the motor again and it began to hum jerkily as we moved off toward our own shoreline. A few hundred yards downstream a German Spandau arched a burst of tracers toward our bank. Then a flare penetrated the darkness, and for five perilous seconds we were left naked and exposed on the middle of the river. A burst of machine-gun bullets spattered the water where we had been. Then another flare burst upon the darkness, but we had already gained the shadow of the summer dike and were safe.

On the river side of the summer dike we saw a German rubber dinghy lying on the bank. Evidently the Germans were on patrol to our side tonight. As we passed by the dinghy, Kettley reached over and pulled it out into the stream and set it adrift.

Lieutenant Cronyn was on the summer dike to guide us in, and we portaged our canoe and began the journey back to the winter dike.

Back in the big white house everyone thawed out and ate a fine meal prepared by our Dutch helpers. It had been a very cold night on the river and I wondered how Leo and Pete had fared. That morning they did not return.

Two days later Pete came on the air on schedule from Tiel. It was a thrilling moment in our lives. Communications were perfect. Secret information began to flow out from enemy-occupied territory. Their information was invaluable to the Army.

Operations on the Waal were now finished for the winter and I moved back to Nijmegen for a week to replan and re-equip. (It was here that I received the news that Kettley was to return to England. After another month of close friendship he departed, and I was left alone with my little band of Dutchmen.)

Then I moved west to the Biesbosch which is the country threaded by waterways on the western extremity of Holland. It consists of many little islands and marshes and small inlets. And it is full of ancient folklore. Once pirates were supposed to have hidden plunder here while escaping from the British.

Lieutenant Koch was here also with his fellow members of the Dutch Intelligence Service. The Biesbosch was the point of infiltration for Dutch agents, a route for the refugees who came down the river in hundreds on moonless nights, an outlet for Allied airmen who had been kept by the Underground, and a point from where we took off on our boating expeditions to meet the evaders. It was a beehive of activity. And on good nights a brisk ferry schedule was carried on into the enemy lines, with haggling and bargaining for top priority. Since we had the boats and the Dutch Intelligence Service had the guides, the situation usually ended in a compromise.

The guide I used most frequently was a playful, bespectacled man called Kos who was only in our employment because it gave him occasion to visit his friends in Sliedrecht and especially his girlfriend who worked in a hospital supervised by the Germans. Kos liked the life of boatman on the river and delighted in bringing back rolls of microfilm, secret documents and odd bits of paraphernalia handed to him by British agents.

I decided one night to go on patrol in our high-powered speedboat, the motor of which had been silenced to a gentle throb. The speedboat was equipped with twin machine-guns both fore and aft. It was our practice to escort the agents' canoes partway up the Merwede River for protection, and then leave them and make our way back to our harbour in the village of Lage Zwaluwe.

It was on such a night as this we were coming home from escort when we saw a suspicious-looking canoe put quickly into shore at one of the islands known as the Point. We darted into shore after it but we lost it in the shore-mist and did not go too close to the island for fear of being grounded on the rocks. After searching the water in the vicinity for the canoe we decided to turn south toward our harbour. As I turned south I noticed that a thick fog had quickly settled on the river and visibility was limited to the nose of the boat. After half an hour's steady running there was no land to be seen ahead of us and I knew we were lost in the fog. In a few moments we ran aground on a reedy island, full of honking, shrieking wildfowl who were disturbed by our presence.

The boatmen and myself worked during the night, shoving and pushing our boat out to deeper water. But it was no use, the tide had receded too quickly and we were marooned near an island on which the Germans kept several machine-gun posts. During the night I checked the position we were in with our map and decided that we were at least four miles east and north of our harbour.

In the early morning we heard meaningless German shouts and waited for the tide to lift us afloat. About five o'clock in the morning the speedboat righted and began to float. The motor started on the second try and this time we moved by the stars west and south. In a half hour we could see our harbour through the cleared morning air. When we harboured we made our way, wet and dejected, home to bed. Anthony, our faithful Dutch interpreter, had been very worried and, when we returned, he greeted us enthusiastically. We were glad to go to bed in the comparative safety and comfort of our house in Lage Zwaluwe.

Jan Staat for four years had manoeuvred his canoe eight miles against treacherous currents up the channels of the Biesbosch. He was willing to do almost anything for us. And he and his comrades did a job on the Biesbosch only known to few. They went on night after night through years of occupation. If ever any of their people were caught, they underwent a torture which cannot honestly be conceived, and to which a quick death was much preferable.

If one went far enough up the Biesbosch, one could enter into the Merwede River which in turn joined with the Maas. One night we received a signal that there would be six people waiting for us at the Dam which was six miles up river. We were to pick them up when the tide running up met the tide coming down and the waters were still. At such a time a canoe could lightly slip by the German sentries on shore.

When we arrived at our secret harbour there was a slight wind in the air which was whipping tiny waves upon the water. I had decided to use tonight a silent-powered canoe which would tow two paddle canoes behind.

A few moments later Jan Staat, Hood, a Canadian Engineer, and myself made our way out of the inlet into the main stream. The night was moonless, and Jan, using his river sense, kept us out in midstream as we began to pass the first island which held a machine-gun post. A white Verey light whooshed out from the bank, lighted the sky directly above us and landed a few feet from the canoes. We waited for the machine-gun fire, but none came.

After an hour on the river Jan guided the boats toward a small cove half hidden by rushes and undergrowth. Here he told me that he would paddle the last half mile alone to the Dam and bring back the six men. At the Dam there would be some of our men with canoes who would be waiting for us. It would be easy for them to come downstream, and they would have to do little more than steer the canoes in the current.

Before one could approach the Dam it was necessary to pass the Cop Van Land, which was two ragged chunks of land which thrust themselves out into the river. At this point the river was less than a hundred yards across, and there were two German posts here as well. On clear nights you could hear the Germans speaking to their women on the Cop. It began to rain, and Jan took into his memory the landmark we were at and pushed off into the river. He would return within two hours.

Hood and I anchored our canoes to the shore and stretched out upon the smooth, white beach. I heard only the grasses licking the sand and the bullfrogs booming their defiance at the darkness.

Hood was one of the Canadian Engineers who had helped in the evacuation of the paratroopers from Arnhem. He was also one of the Engineers who were working with us. Four months ago Major Neave and myself had borrowed twenty Engineers for two days from the Canadian Army, and they had been with us ever since. Hood was willing to go anywhere, provided he didn't have to go alone. He now had burrowed a hole in the sand and covered up his head while he smoked a cigarette.

Two hours later I squinted my eyes and looked out into the river. I saw three shapeless patches moving across the water toward the beach. The dark shapes changed themselves into canoes. Jan had the people we wanted with him. Jan jumped lightly ashore and wiped the night mist off his glasses with his handkerchief.

"Five men, one woman tonight," he said smiling. "Long Jan says the woman and her man are all right."

I looked into the canoe nearest me. In the back seat sat a woman covered in an ermine evening wrap. In front of her was a man. He turned and looked nervously into the reeds behind me before speaking.

"You people the Canadian Patrol that's supposed to be meeting us?"

I told him we were. It was a rich American voice from somewhere in the southern States.

Jan had the boats tied together now, and Hood turned over the motor, and we began to purr away down the Merwede in the darkness. As we passed the island where the Germans had shot a flare at us we only saw mist and darkness. And the soft whimpering of our motor was the only sound in the night.

Half an hour later, moored again at our base in Hooge Zwalue (a little Dutch village on the Merwede River) I took the six evaders back to my house and for the first time saw them in the light.

Two were British paratroop survivors from Arnhem, who had travelled seventy miles across Holland with the Dutch Underground in order to arrive at the Dam tonight. One was a British pilot who had escaped from a German prison camp after two years of captivity. He was soft spoken and seemed mild. The other pilot was an American from Georgia, who had been hidden by the Dutch for seven months around Rotterdam.

Then there was the lady from Amsterdam in the evening wrap, corduroy trousers and long tresses. She was an attractive woman of about thirty. She had a deep tan. The pouches of her cheeks were full, and she was well fed. The man she said was her husband, was tall, blond, very thin, and played the piano while he waited. His name was Olaf.

Sergeant Needhoff, who worked with me as a linguist, remarked at the time that Olaf spoke Dutch with a slight German intonation and occasionally let slip into his conversation a German expression. The Dutchman and the woman told me they were fleeing from the S.D. (which was the Dutch secret police). We knew, however, that the Dutch S.D. was the organization whose job it was to penetrate the Dutch Resistance. Yet Long Jan had sent them to us, and we trusted Long Jan.

After we dined our guests, we prepared to take them by automobile on the next stage of their journey. I kept thinking of the two Dutch civilians, and decided that they would go to our Counter-Espionage office for interrogation. It was fortunate they did. Two weeks later their results reached me. The lady had held a high position in the Dutch Quisling Party and the man had been her dupe. Both, knowing that their cause was a lost one and being aware that for them there was no road back, had managed to penetrate the Dutch Underground and had attempted to pass themselves as Dutch refugees.

On dark moonless nights, hundreds of refugees would stream out of the Biesbosch down the black river towards our lines. Night after night rowboats filled with families kept coming down. And the old skippers, who guided them down the eight miles of river, would spit on their coarse hands, and row back to the Dam the same night and return to their homes in occupied Holland. Until, finally, one night the Germans sank a row of barges across the Merwede, and it seemed as if no boats could come down any more.

But the people were not discouraged. When the Germans would plug up one channel, the Dutch skippers would find another channel. And when that was plugged up, there would still be others which could be used. If all the channels were blocked, then the Underground would blow the obstacles and the skippers would go through again. These people wanted their freedom, and when people want their freedom, you cannot stop them from doing anything.

I remember Pete, the blond youth who rowed me across the Waal. Pete has rowed to safety many men who were hunted and seeking refuge. But now Pete is dead, shot by the Gestapo, and his true name is not even known to his associates.

There was Jop, the small blond young man who was put in a concentration camp by the Germans. He saw his brother tortured before his eyes. And when he escaped he vowed to kill Germans. He has done much more than that. He has kept the spirit of Holland living through four years of adversity. (I met him at Maurik after I had been rowed across the Rhine by the Underground.)

There is Kos, my guide in the Biesbosch, who removed charges from a dike and prevented a large area of Holland from being immediately inundated. Two months ago I met Kos in London where he was recovering from an accident in Holland. He was lonely and forgotten.

There were Leo and Pete, whom I have already mentioned. They were pioneers in a new means of secret communication.

Three months after the completion of their operation Leo's mutilated body was found on the river bank of the Waal. Pete, we discovered, had been taken as a prisoner to Germany for forced labour.

I am proud to call all these men my close friends, and our association through the months of Holland's subjugation is something which I will never forget.

There were many Leos, Peters, Jans, and Jops; and words sometimes can fail to tell of their great courage, devotion and the principles by which they lived. When they lived there was the wild freedom of Holland in their hearts, and when they died it was always with the thought of a Free Netherlands in their minds.

Tex Banwell made one last attempt to gain freedom on a freezing winter night in January. Out of the ten members who began this trip across the Rhine, three survived the long, hazardous journey over icy dikes, snowy ground, and flooded, frozen land to our lines. Somewhere on the route Tex separated from the rest of his party when they were ambushed by the Germans, and today he is a repatriated prisoner of war.

Many of the Underground workers are now occupying key positions in the Netherlands Government. There was Captain Tromp of the Dutch Resistance, whom I had close associations with. One day in Eindhoven I asked to see Captain Tromp at his office. "Captain Tromp," the woman said. "He is the Minister of Waterways now, in London."

For some the story had a happy ending.

It was February when I was recalled from the Biesbosch and told to head east with the assault forces into Germany and Holland, the idea being that once a breakthrough was accomplished, I was to reach our contact men in eastern Holland. From them I would find where some Arnhem survivors and airmen were in hiding.

A few days before I was to participate in the Rhine crossing, Kettley and myself, out of curiosity more than anything else, accompanied parts of the Canadian Infantry assault across flooded land east of Nijmegen almost to the border of Germany.

We arrived at the launching-point in time to catch a Buffalo (a huge amphibious tank which can carry fifty men) across the flooded area to the dike road where the attack went in along. On the dike road were the deserted trenches of the Germans who had fled when the first Buffalos had crossed.

After an hour of walking on the dike road, we overtook the leading Infantry, and marched along the road with them. The country was very flat. Suddenly Kettley wandered off to a solitary barn about fifty feet off the road to our right, and reappeared from its interior accompanied by twenty Germans all waving white flags. Kettley pocketed a German revolver which he took from one of the prisoners, gave me one, and handed the Germans over to the troops, and we resumed our march.

We soon entered a deserted and shattered Dutch village which lay practically on the German border. Here Kettley and I left the Infantry troops and began to wander about the village, curious to see what it held. After a few minutes we came upon some more of our own troops in position, facing us from the second storey of several houses. Then I was suddenly confronted by an enormous man who must have been over six foot three in height and who weighed more than three hundred pounds. He drew a revolver on me and pointed it at my heart.

"Don't you recognize me, Ben?" I said. "I'm Leo Heaps."

"Well, I'll be a son of a — !" His revolver began to falter and he put it down. "How? Where? How can it be you? What are you doing here? Show me your identification! I don't believe it!" Then began a string of happy oaths. Ben was glad to see me again. This was Major Ben Dunkelman, D.S.O., a very close friend of mine from Toronto. Since I was dirty, unshaven and unkempt he had not recognized me quite as quickly as I had recognized him. I explained to him what I was doing in this part of the world.

The rest of the day Kettley and I spent with Ben, marching toward Germany. Occasionally we would stop to place a guard over a German supply dump. When we crossed the border we discovered nothing more interesting than several German deserters who surrendered, and a big German quartermaster store piled high with supplies. The few people we did see in Germany trembled with fear and expected rapine, torture and death. All we did was to take a little of their plentiful food stock for an evening meal. After this their fear subsided, and we returned into Holland for the night. Since our feet were very wet everybody took a pair of German jackboots from the quartermaster store. All that night we remained with Ben, and in the early dawn we wished each other goodbye, and Kettley and I tried to make arrangements for a ride by any sort of vehicle to Nijmegen. It was impossible. The Germans had blown a dike to our east and the water had risen to several feet on the roads; no vehicle could get through. The only way we could return to Nijmegen was to walk four miles along the gale-swept dike, and then catch a Buffalo back across a mile of flooded land.

I was informed that as far as I was concerned the Rhine crossing would be postponed. Instead, I would remain in

Holland. After two days of waiting I wandered off with Anthony, my interpreter, and Deis, the jeep-driver, into north-east Holland.

We drove for a day northward up the east bank of the Ijssel River until we passed our rear troops, and then we turned east into north-eastern Holland. The enemy situation was very fluid, and there would be opportunity to operate five to ten miles ahead of our Infantry.

There was a Dutch major on Prince Bernhard's staff who travelled around with a chauffeur in a 1937 Buick coupe. His name was Schoutin. He spoke in such rapid Dutch that it was difficult to follow him. He was a small man who did everything with rapid motions, and for protection he carried a small .32 pistol which always failed to fire when it was needed most.

Working with me I had a troop of four reconnaissance cars. One day we advanced into the outskirts of a town called Doetinchem, firing bursts from our machine-guns at the odd Germans who were popping in and out of houses and running across fields.

I had a rendezvous at a water-tower about fifty feet in front of me with some evaders. I stopped my jeep in front of it.

Off the road to the left there was something that looked like a camouflaged gun pointing in my direction. Schoutin pooh-poohed the idea. I fired at it anyway, to make certain. To our amazement thirty Germans appeared out of slit-trenches and surrendered to us. When I inspected the German slit-trenches I discovered an eighty-eight millimetre gun pointed directly at my parked jeep, and the gun was loaded. It was very fortunate for us that they had decided to surrender.

Our store of German loot began to pile up. Deis had a pair of wristwatches on each wrist, and two Lugers stuck in his belt. The rest of us did pretty well too.

That afternoon in the little side-streets of Doetinchem I lost the reconnaissance cars, and I proceeded with the indomitable Schoutin behind me in the Buick coupe. A few Germans ran in and out of houses twenty-five feet ahead of us. We sprayed them with our Vickers. Ahead was the telephone exchange which would be a valuable prize if we could capture it intact. As our jeep moved towards it a lone German on a bicycle swerved out of the yard and peddled furiously away. Anthony placed his Tommy-gun on his shoulder and fired at him. The German escaped by turning a corner farther down the road. Then with a terrific explosion the telephone exchange blew up, and pieces of timber, bricks and masonry flew in all directions into the air. The Germans had beaten us to it.

We retraced our tracks and returned to the outskirts of Doetinchem to meet the forward Infantry battalions coming up to occupy the ground. The Infantry moved slowly on foot, and where swift vehicles can pass through thinly dispersed enemy, the Infantry usually arrive to meet a prepared enemy. Such was the case in Doetinchem where our Infantrymen suffered casualties from mortaring and machine-gun fire.

I met my brother who came up with the Infantry and it was very nice to see him again. That night we slept at the Burgomaster's house.

Next morning I contacted some pilots who had been hiding in a houseboat on the Ijssel River and they returned with me to Doetinchem.

Major Schoutin had decided to remain in Doetinchem for a meeting with members of the Underground. In the afternoon my jeep went ahead alone towards the neighbouring town of Ulf, which had not yet been visited by Allied troops. Half an hour's driving took us into the main part of Ulf where we slowly drove through the deserted streets. In the distance a

German Volkswagen Kübelwagen (a poor imitation of the jeep) was fleeing down a country road. Anthony remarked that Major Schoutin had arrived in his coupe and was following us.

Presently one or two frightened civilians came to their doorways and waved to us. Soon more people came to the doorways and the braver ones ventured out on the streets. Some began to shout when the realization that the Germans had gone penetrated their brains. Then the crowds poured out upon the streets, shouting and waving. The Dutch flag magically appeared on balconies and the jeep and the coupe were mobbed. We were hoisted high. People danced on the streets cheering and yelling. Some of the Dutchmen were examining the Buick coupe, not certain what peculiar powers it held. Anthony was crowned with a wreath of flowers and was trying to give cigarettes away without being knocked down from his pedestal on the jeep. The Dutch had not seen cigarettes for four years. Major Schoutin was proclaiming that he represented Prince Bernhard, and the shouts of the Dutchmen became more jubilant. All that day we celebrated in Ulf and when night came we watched the collaborators being brought in by the Underground. That night the town bishop invited us to his diocese and we were feasted on huge slices of pork and beef, young chickens, creamy desserts and rare wines. I mentally compared this to the black bread, thin soups, and the occasional piece of bacon the remainder of the people ate.

Next morning the reconnaissance cars arrived and we were no longer the only troops in Ulf.

Major Schoutin returned to Eindhoven to see Prince Bernhard, and I returned to our temporary headquarters in Zutphen which was on the bank of the Ijssel River.

The next two days we spent re-equipping ourselves for the

assault across the Ijssel with the First Canadian Division. We were to cross with one specially armoured jeep and a duckling (an amphibious jeep) and try to link up the small group of paratroops dropped twenty miles east to work with the Underground.

Next night my two vehicles gathered at the concentration area near Zutphen ready for the crossing. The duckling crossed the river under its own power and the jeep was loaded onto a water buffalo. It was two o'clock in the morning when we were across, and we camped for the night close to the bank among the Infantry slit-trenches. In the morning we moved on with the Infantry to more forward positions.

While we were waiting for a further move by our troops the Germans began to mortar the forward observation house we were in. Anthony, the interpreter, was hit by a piece of flying shrapnel. Then the Engineer who drove the duckling was seriously wounded and they both had to be evacuated.

I returned to our headquarters in Zutphen to report on the situation. When I arrived at Zutphen I was told that I would join a Special Air Service squadron which was ready to strike across the Rhine into Arnhem. We rested for a day and then left early next morning for Elst, which lay directly across the Rhine from Arnhem. I would now be returning to familiar ground. It was now the month of April and spring was beginning to spice the air.

Henry Druce was the Major commanding the Special Air Service Squadron. He had flown small observation planes into France to land and pick up Agents two years before D-Day. Five months before the invasion of France began Henry operated his jeep squadron all the way from the Forest of the Ardennes to the coast of the Riviera. He was long experienced in work deep in the interior of enemy territory, and under these conditions he felt at home. His jeeps were each mounted with five machine-guns, carried armour-plating for protection and had two specially built-in gasoline tanks. Each jeep had a wireless set. Our expedition would have sixteen jeeps, and fifty-three men.

Henry met me in Elst the evening before we were to cross into Arnhem.

"Hello, Leo, old man, so awfully glad to see you! Should be quite a party," he remarked lightly. He was dressed in corduroy trousers, wore a battle jacket minus his many decorations and insignias, and perched upon his head he had an old top hat which he grew to love as an old friend as the days passed by; on his feet he wore a pair of American jumping boots.

"We intended to jump, you know, but Captain Holland's party jumped last night instead. We'll infiltrate and link up with old Holland. Will he be surprised to see us!" he chortled. (Captain Holland and Captain Knottenbelt both had a party of men who had parachuted into central Holland three days ago.)

Next morning we moved across the pontoon bridge into Arnhem. Arnhem was a shattered town. Everything standing was at least partially destroyed. Every house had been ransacked by the Germans in their search for the paratroops eight months ago. The town itself which once contained ninety thousand people was now deserted except for our Infantry and our jeep convoy which moved cautiously through the streets.

Henry and I visited a Reconnaissance Squadron which had just arrived and found everything thoroughly confused. No one knew what the next move was. But it became apparent during the next hour that the Fifth Canadian Armoured Division was moving in with its tanks, and we knew that if we didn't move out quickly our role would be duplicated by the

143

tanks and we would be out of a job. Henry didn't want to miss the thrill of liberating western Holland. Neither did I. That night we moved off in the darkness north and west toward Barneveld. All that night our progress was delayed by roadblocks and Germans, most of whom were Dutch SS troops which we took prisoner. In the morning a Canadian tank column overtook us and we followed the tanks.

Our maps showed a German artillery Regiment emplaced upon a wooded hill ten miles north-west of Arnhem near a crossroad.

Henry remarked, "I guess those eighty-eights aren't around here any more." Just then we approached the crossroad. Henry's oaths were drowned out by the whine of many shells bursting about twenty-five yards to our left. Then the shells began to close in until they were bursting among our jeeps. The tankmen could put their heads in the turrets and disappear into the safety of the tanks, but our flimsily-armoured jeeps had no protection. The shelling was terrifying and deadly and everyone in the jeeps vanished into the slit-trenches beside the road. Henry didn't mind being behind the lines, but being in front of the enemy was an entirely new proposition and it meant organized warfare with all its artillery and regularity of mortaring. During a second or two of silence we boarded our jeeps again and tore down a side road away from the lumbering tanks. It was almost miraculous that neither jeep nor man was injured. A half mile back we could hear the shells whining over our heads and then crashing on the crossroads.

I sent out a jeep ahead to reconnoitre a road through. An hour later we received a message over the wireless to meet it at a position several miles west from us. When we reached the appointed place we rode still farther on until we stopped at a house near a main crossroad several miles west from where we had been. Here once again we sent a patrol ahead and this time the patrol came back with half a dozen Germans who were found indifferently laying telephone cable when they were picked up by our men. They were happy to be taken prisoner.

Eric, the Dutchman who had taken Anthony's place as interpreter, had meanwhile discovered a civilian in a house who turned out to be a Dutch SS Stormtrooper in hiding. Without a moment's hesitation Eric picked up a silent Sten gun, dragged the SS man away behind the house and shot him dead. Then two men picked up shovels and buried the SS trooper.

That night several Germans, quite lost and wandering, came across our position and were taken prisoner. The night otherwise was uneventful.

Next morning when we advanced again we approached a large main highway running from Barneveld to Amersfoort. Henry and I crept up to the road to see if it was clear, and as we looked down the road to our right we saw advancing, not more than half a mile off, a column of German Infantry numbering about forty men. I went back and called up six jeeps, and placed them in the bushes beside the main road in position for an ambush. When the Germans came abreast of the jeeps the Vickers guns would cut them to ribbons. We trained twenty-four machine-guns upon twenty feet of road. Presently Henry signalled, the Germans were only a hundred yards away. Henry crawled ten feet back from the road to where I was. I had a dreadful feeling in my stomach that the Germans would see the jeeps. Then came a terrific steady burst of bullets from our guns and Germans began toppling over on the road. All the reply we received was one lone German bullet which went between Henry and myself. As we turned our jeeps around and raced away, I thought of the dog-tired soldier who led the column. He had turned around and spun as he fell. It was too dramatic.

After travelling five miles north-west through a lightly wooded forest we parked on the quiet lawn of a hospital ground and set up our wireless. Henry and I sent two messages back to London, and then prepared to move again north toward Barneveld in case the Germans began to follow our jeep tracks in real earnest.

That evening before dusk we ran our jeeps into a little clump of woods, but before we had time to settle down to eat, several German patrols were sighted headed our way. We were an easy target in the isolated wood so we moved off again still farther north and west and arrived at dusk at what was once a German training ground. We stopped for a hurried meal.

It was not long before we heard the bellowing of German voices and the sound of horse-drawn transport moving by quite close to our encampment. Near me I heard a sharp scuffle for a second or two, then silence. One of our men had just captured a stray German who had wandered off from his company. Promptly the interpreters pumped him with questions. It was discovered that we were wedged between two German regiments which were moving east into the attack against our forward elements in Otterlo. This was no place for us to be. In the meantime several more stray Germans wandered into the woods we were in and were also taken prisoner by our sentries. The prisoners were put on our jeeps and we prepared to move. By this time it was really dark and the only light was a bit of moon which glowed through thick cloud layers. Now something happened which was typical of the fearlessness of Henry Druce. With him at the head of the column and my jeep directly behind his, we drove onto the road where the Germans advanced east in single file, and sped on by them without a shot being fired, or cry being sounded.

After half an hour's driving we left the Germans well behind. I noticed that the land we were on was growing leveller and the earth was changing to sand. Soon the track we were on disappeared into a land of scrubby bushes and sand, which seemed to stretch to the horizon. It was something akin, I imagine, to the Nairobi Desert. Henry stopped the jeep column and came over to me.

"You better take over the column, my compass doesn't work too well."

We consulted the map and discovered we were on a wasteland in central Holland. To the north about forty miles distant was a wood and solid ground, which led in turn to a main road not many miles from Stroe. Barneveld, the town we wanted to reach, was about 20 miles west of Stroe.

All that night and morning our jeep column moved by compass north-west, up and down sand dunes and across sand which half enveloped the jeep wheels; but still they went on and in early morning we struck the woods. Our jeeps ploughed straight through the outer fringes of the woods until we came upon a cart track. Here the vehicles fell into column, and everybody stopped for rest and food.

Shortly after dawn we moved further into the woods, occasionally surprising a stray German wandering about aimlessly and lost. Once we came upon a German half-track vehicle, which two German mechanics were working upon. When they saw our jeeps appear from around a bend in the path they threw their tools into the air and with a "*Kamerad*", they vanished almost instantly into the woods. After another hour of driving we drove our jeeps off the track we were on and hid them among the bushes. Then patrols were sent out to scout the surrounding area.

When the patrols returned it was almost night and too late to move again. One patrol had returned with the news that Barneveld was already liberated and the ground ahead was occupied by our own troops. If this was the case then we were wasting our time hiding from non-existent Germans. But since Dutch civilian reports in the past few days had not proven accurate we were inclined to disbelieve such rumours. During the night we heard the heavy clanking of tanks and took care not to attract too much attention in case they were German.

In the new day we moved off in a cold, miserable dawn. When we began to approach Barneveld we passed our own tanks which were off to the side of the road for lack of gasoline to go any farther. When we reached Barneveld itself, Canadian Military Policemen were directing traffic. Then, as if to heap even greater shame upon us, we saw a sign which pointed to Divisional Headquarters. Even Divisional Headquarters had arrived before us. Henry and I hung our heads in shame as we drove through the town.

Later on in the morning we did, however, bring back some pilots who were still hiding to the north of Barneveld in an area which had not been visited by our troops. Then Henry met Captain Holland and his party who had dropped by parachute three days ago, and who seemed to have done nothing more than live in the best Dutch homes until the Canadian tanks reached them.

In Barneveld I saw Major Neave and Major Fraser with the long trail of Dutchmen who followed them about. They as usual were quite comfortable, living in the former Burgomaster's house after he had been arrested as a Quisling. Here I met Dick Kragt, an Englishman of Dutch extraction, who had been in the employment of Major Neave, and had parachuted into Holland over two and a half years ago to facilitate the evacuation of many airmen and Dutchmen who were in hiding. Dick Kragt was a corporal in the Intelligence Corps and was a man of courage. I had heard much about him, and now I met him.

I bid Henry Druce goodbye that morning, and he left, still wearing his top hat, for Nijmegen.

During the next week Dick Kragt and I motored over north-west Holland meeting old acquaintances who had helped me through the lines over seven months ago.

After a pleasant vacation on the Zuider Zee I returned to Barneveld. Orders were awaiting me to move into central Germany. I was to go with a Canadian called Captain Gray. We were to move into Germany almost immediately.

III: BELSEN

DURING MY STAY in Germany the role we were told to play was hindered by the lack of sympathetic people on the land; which made it necessary to advance with the forward elements of our troops. It is of one particular day in Germany that I would like to write about now. On this day I witnessed a sight so horrible and unbelievable that in later times it was difficult to conceive in memory the things I actually saw.

We had been advancing east in central Germany one day in April, and had been warned of a German concentration camp in the area. A little later we came upon the barbed-wire perimeter which surrounded it, and upon a huge enclosure of planks rimmed with more strands of barbed wire. Troops had evidently been here before us, for signs saying "Beware of Typhus" were everywhere. I noticed on the side entrance that Hungarians were on guard. We went in the entrance with our jeep. The Hungarians were very servile. They had been employed by the Germans to do the duty guards. We passed through another gate and we were into the main part of Belsen. The sight I saw made me suck in my breath.

Lying all over the ground there were bodies, thin and emaciated. There were thousands of them. They looked as thin as dried leaves. Some people were crawling on their bellies past us, others were relieving themselves anywhere. The faces of the people were shrivelled and were drawn like tight sheets of paper about shrunken skulls. But it was the eyes of the children which frightened you. Small, dark eyes that seemed almost to have disappeared back into the recesses of the brain. Their eyes were duller than mist and as transparent. No one paid any attention to us. There seemed to be no German guards inside the camp.

As we passed some of the people tried to raise their faces upward in ugly grimaces. They were trying to smile at us. Most lacked the strength to look up.

It was difficult to tell the dead on the ground from the living. If a body quivered, you knew it was in the last stages of life. If it remained still for an hour or more, it was sure to be dead either from typhus or starvation.

I saw two tiny, wasted figures carry a third out of a hut and lay it down upon the ground. You could see this happening every few minutes.

A little distance away another wizened figure was pushing a wheelbarrow. Inside there was the remains of what was a boy. He lay crumpled like dust in the bottom of the wheelbarrow, and his big, swollen head would wobble feebly in protest as the wheelbarrow jogged along.

Each figure that walked, stumbled along with the weariness of the living dead, plodding through hell. Each step one of these figures took was filled with terrible agony.

Everywhere the dead lay rotting, and every now and then a live man would lie down to die beside his dead mate.

We passed one of the huts where the people lived. The stench of diseased life was overpowering. It engulfed you. We had to move away. But we could see people lying side by side, across and over one another and nude on the floor.

If hell has a counterpart, it was here.

We passed the great pits where the dead, like twigs, lay stacked upon the dead. There were countless thousands in the pits.

On the edge of the camp the more recent arrivals lived. They lived in family groups, with almost always a woman who cooked in charge. What they cooked, I don't know.

It was a huge camp. Some men say there were as many as fifty thousand people in the camp. Others say no one will ever know how many lived and died there. I saw some of our soldiers in rubber suits spraying and decontaminating the shacks.

I stopped and spoke to a corporal. He told me they had arrived a few hours before, and had immediately put the SS women and guards in the camp jail. The Commandant, a Major Kramer, was kept in special solitary confinement. I visited these people. When I saw them they were craven and very servile. Only last night, out of sheer brutality, they had shot fifteen helpless inmates dead.

I looked at these beasts, who had once been men. They winced and withdrew into the shadows of their cell. No matter how degraded they had forced, by starvation and indignity, the people of the camp to become, the SS guards had reached by their own crimes untouchable depths of degradation. These men were the untouchables. They were fed on crusts of black bread and three slices of bully beef a day. They were all stripped to the waist and stank of sweat.

Outside an old white-haired lady looked up at us and said, "Please give me a cigarette. Don't be angry if I ask. Don't be angry." She was beyond thinness.

We gave her all we had. Habit had made her expect a beating where she should have received kindness. Who knows from what home she had been dragged, what luxury of age she had been denied, what wealth she had been stripped of? And now she was reduced to this.

Everywhere it was the same. Here in a cesspool of disease and filth the best brains of the country lay rotting, the best men lay stewing in their own juices — professors, clergymen and ordinary people.

I saw the gas chamber where every day fifty men, women and children were put to death by lethal gas in a series of experiments carried on by an eminent German scientist. I saw the incinerators where the dead and the living were burned. And then I saw where the red cabbages grew out of the fertilization of human ashes.

It was appalling to think that human beings had calculatingly designed this camp to destroy their own kind.

Everything I saw here was scientifically designed to degrade intelligent human beings, by indignity and starvation, to the state of beasts. To the gas chamber, where a Dr. Stein experimented in various lethal gases, to the pits stacked high with the dead, everything was coldly and mathematically planned to the last detail. The same number that died must be replaced by the same number of living new arrivals.

The Nazis had succeeded. They had reduced the inmates to the state of beasts.

At the main gate a medical officer stopped us. I stripped, and was sprayed from head to foot with anti-typhus powder. Then I dressed again.

At the main gate we met a very pretty Hungarian woman. She was also an inmate, but was in much better health than the others. She spoke English fluently and was acting as an interpreter.

She told me that she had been studying physics in Hungary, but during the war had been forced, because of anti-Semitic decrees, to study economics. She had obtained her degree. And when the Germans had taken over complete control of

Hungary, she had been pressed into service with one of the labour gangs. Here the food was almost sufficient to live on, and with what she could get by bribing the guards, she had managed to keep her health. Two weeks ago she had been brought to Belsen. Her great crime in life was that she was Jewish. There was no malice in her voice as she spoke. She seemed to have infinite tolerance for others. Only her eyes told of her intolerable loneliness.

We watched the inmates in their striped pyjama uniforms trying to move from one hut to another. They would wobble a few feet, then stop, then wobble again and stop, until they reached the next building. Here they would pause for rest, completely exhausted. The distance between two huts could not have been more than ten feet.

"Some food is being brought in now," she said. "Perhaps some of the people will be saved. Already the dead are being separated from the living, and the doomed from those who will survive. Those who are not diseased and able to walk are to be moved as quickly as possible to another camp."

The young woman told me how much crueller the SS women were than the SS male guards. And how she had used her feminine wiles to secure food from the guard who supervised her hut.

Her fiancé was in Hungary. He was all she had left in the world, and she was clinging desperately to the hope that he still lived and that they would some day meet again. This woman was only twenty-one years of age.

Stimpson, the driver of my jeep, had just finished being deloused. We said goodbye to the Hungarian woman and left.

Stimpson is a plain, good-natured Canadian from the west. He is hardened to the ways of war, and he has seen a great deal of the privation and suffering in Europe. But all that night as

154

we drove Stimpson kept repeating to me, "You know, people who treat other people like that can't be human. They *can't* be human."

Stimpson was right.

We could not eat anything that evening.

And the last thing I saw before my eyes that night was the ghoulish picture of the dead who walked alone in hell.

Later on in the month of April I returned to my headquarters — which was now located in a little villa near Barneveld in Holland — and was given the latest details of the battle. Everywhere the Germans were giving themselves up. Already negotiations for unconditional surrender were going on between the Dutch Government and the Germans in the northern, occupied part of Holland. My work was now finished.

On a damp, dreary afternoon in late April Stimpson drove me to the airport. Here I took a last look at the familiar canals and windmills that lay scattered on the land as far as my eye could see. Then I boarded my aeroplane for England.

Now I am aboard a great ocean liner which is taking me daily closer and closer to Canada. My experiences of the past nine months seem very far away. Already the land they took place in is assuming to me the memory of a strange country, and the people are appearing as a foreign people. Yet my true friends are in Holland.

The war in Europe is over. The Germans have gone and now all of Europe must be revived and brought back to health again. The people of the Underground, who during the war risked their lives at the most hazardous tasks, have now returned quietly to their homes. Their job today is as great as it was, only now there is a long road ahead to lasting peace.

A great new door in life had opened for me, and I had stepped in over the magic threshold. I was now wise enough to know how colossal was my ignorance of life.

Then I went on deck to watch the shores of my native land loom up ahead. Soon I would be home again.

A NOTE TO THE READER

If you have enjoyed this book enough to leave a review on **Amazon** and **Goodreads**, then we would be truly grateful.
Sapere Books

Sapere Books is an exciting new publisher of brilliant fiction and popular history.

To find out more about our latest releases and our monthly bargain books visit our website:
saperebooks.com

Made in the USA
Las Vegas, NV
13 November 2023

80735827R00087